WILLIAMS-SONOMA

entertaining
with the seasons

FREE PRESS

NEW YORK · LONDON · TORONTO · SYDNEY

contents

ONE OF LIFE'S GREAT JOYS is gathering company around the table to share good food and conversation. Part of the pleasure is in the cooking, knowing you've prepared the best of what's in season for your friends and family. The dishes you make don't have to be elaborate, fussy, or complicated. In fact, simple preparations often show off flavors best—and allow you to spend more time with your guests. One of my fondest memories is of an impromptu dinner party one recent spring evening when by chance all my grown children were home at the same time. I hadn't planned a dinner, but when I asked if they'd like to stay, they all said, "Of course!" and continued their conversations. I had arborio rice in the pantry, prosciutto and Parmesan in the refrigerator, and fresh peas and fava beans, so I made a large pot of creamy risotto and garnished it with pan-fried prosciutto. The conversation and camaraderie went on as we lingered over wine and the season's first strawberries.

Of course some gatherings do require more advance planning, such as a summer cocktail party or a special occasion dinner. And for those times, having a strategy helps. For a Thanksgiving feast, I start a day or two ahead, toasting nuts and making pies. The evening before, I set the table and decorate. I'm up early the next morning, roasting the turkey and preparing the rest of the meal. By the time guests arrive, I'm relaxed and happy to welcome them with a glass of Champagne and a tray of appetizers. During the dark midwinter evenings, I love to invite friends over for a cozy dinner in front of the brick fireplace in my kitchen. As guests arrive, they're lured to the kitchen by the aroma of braised short ribs. While we enjoy wine with olives and toasted almonds, I finish a salad of oranges plucked from my trees, avocado, and shaved fennel. For dessert, I'll serve a compote of dried fruit I made the day before with biscotti—and some warming port to finish the evening.

I hope the recipes in this book will inspire you to cook with the seasons throughout the year, and share many great meals with friends and family. No matter what the occasion, serving simply prepared and delicious food ensures a good time—and after all, isn't that the point of entertaining?

Georgeanne Brennan

ENTERTAINING is about sharing good food and drinks with friends and family. And whether you're hosting a casual dinner or an elegant cocktail fete, the experience can be fun and easy when you keep it simple and seasonal. With proper planning, fresh ingredients, and inspired presentation ideas, you'll be ready to host any type of gathering.

The key to a successful dinner party is to stay organized by breaking down the work of planning, shopping, and cooking into manageable, do-ahead tasks. In this book, you'll find recipes for every season, along with some suggested menus, to mix and match as you wish.

Planning the Menu

When hosting a party, it's helpful to avoid the urge to be too ambitious—as tempting as it might be. As you plan your menu, start simple and build from there, always with an eye toward the seasons and foods that can be prepared or assembled ahead of time to limit last-minute attention.

Seasonality and Balance

As any chef will tell you, seasonality is the most important guideline in planning a menu. In-season ingredients offer the best flavor and often the best prices. Fresh produce, prepared simply, is ideal for entertaining any time of year. Dishes like crisp salad greens drizzled with vinaigrette, roasted asparagus, or a rustic fruit galette are often just as pleasing, attractive, and flavorful as more elaborate and time-consuming preparations.

Think about dishes that match the weather, too: a grilled entree with a light salad on a warm summer evening, a hearty braised dish with polenta on a fall or winter night.

Aim to plan a menu that offers a variety of colors, textures, and flavors. Consider the menu as a whole and choose complementary and contrasting elements. Balance a rich starter with a light main course, or a chilled soup or small salad with a more substantial main dish. Keep individual flavors focused and simple, so that each element of the meal has its own distinctive character.

Keep it Simple

Give some thought to the realities of your kitchen, your skill level, your budget, and your schedule. The larger the guest list, the less complicated your menu should be. Choose dishes that can be made in advance (you'll want to prepare as much as possible before guests arrive), and don't hesitate to use some high-quality store-bought ingredients, such as spreads and sauces, antipasti, or even a dessert from a favorite local bakery. Have store-bought salty snacks on hand to serve with drinks when your guests first arrive.

GENERAL SUPPLIES TO HAVE ON HAND FOR ENTERTAINING

Outfitting your home and pantry with a few well-chosen basics will make any dinner party easier:

- Serving platters, trays, bowls, boards, pitchers, and carafes
- Small dishes and bowls; cheese board, knives, and spreaders
- Candles (votives, pillars, and tapers), vases, and place cards
- Ice bucket, corkscrew, coasters, and cocktail napkins
- Nuts (almonds, cashews, peanuts, pistachios, and spiced walnuts); jars of olives; tapenade and other spreads
- Crackers, flatbreads, and bread sticks; tortilla chips and salsa

THE PARTY PANTRY

Setting out a variety of savory tidbits ahead of time is a great idea—your guests will have something to nibble on with drinks as soon as they arrive. Allow chilled items to come to room temperature for the best flavor. And don't forget to set out a small dish for olive pits and nut shells. The following quick-to-assemble appetizers feature store-bought items.

Crostini Spread thin toasted baguette rounds with olive tapenade or onion jam, or layer with fresh ricotta or goat cheese and prosciutto.

Marcona Almonds Look for these Spanish blanched almonds, sold roasted with oil and salt, at specialty-food markets; toss with coarsely chopped rosemary sprigs and/or red pepper flakes.

Bocconcini Skewer these bite-sized balls of fresh mozzarella with cherry tomatoes and fresh basil leaves on decorative picks.

Edamame These fresh soybeans, cooked in the pod, are sold in the freezer section of most supermarkets; boil and serve with coarse sea salt.

Olives Dress up jarred olives or a mix of favorites from an olive bar by tossing them with olive oil, minced herbs, and lemon or orange zest.

Salumi Buy thinly sliced Italian cured meats, such as coppa and salami. Plan on about 1 ounce (30 g) total per guest. Roll each slice and arrange the slices on a platter; serve with crackers or bread sticks.

Meze Platter Set out bowls of hummus, baba ghanoush, stuffed grape leaves, and olives. Cut a stack of pita bread into wedges or strips and serve alongside in a napkin-lined basket.

Shopping Tips

Today's farmers' markets, grocery stores, and specialty-food shops offer more fresh ingredients, as well as prepared items, than ever. The key is to shop strategically.

Plan Ahead

Aim to finish most of your shopping at least a day before the party, leaving only a few items to the last minute. Save time by calling ahead and reserving major purchases, like meat, fish, or wine, so your order is ready to pick up. Ask for items to be as fully prepared as possible: meats trimmed, tied, or sliced; fish boned and filleted; oysters shucked and packed on ice.

Look for Time Savers

As you shop, make mental notes of products that can save you time, like vacuum-packed precooked beets, cut-up fruits, prewashed greens, shaved Parmesan cheese, and peeled and deveined shrimp. These types of products can cut out recipe steps and prep time without compromising flavor and finished appearance.

Purchasing one or more courses can make a huge difference in the amount of time it takes to put together a meal. Build up a "library" of options that will work for entertaining. Look for fully prepared items such as stuffed olives, pasta or potato salads, sliced cured meats, home-style pies or tarts, or local chocolates and cookies. Serve them just as they are, arranged on plates, or add a garnish—a fresh herb sprig, a splash of olive oil, a sprinkle of shredded cheese, a dollop of whipped cream, or a handful of fresh berries.

Planning the Drinks

A dinner party calls for well-selected wines and fun, creative beverages, from colorful cocktails to refreshing coolers. It's always welcoming to greet guests with an aperitif, such as Prosecco or Campari and soda, served with salty snacks, like olives or nuts. When planning, begin with the basics: red and white wine or rosé; still and sparkling water; and, for casual meals, beer.

About Wine

Select wines that will pair well with the food you're serving. Ask your local wine merchant for recommendations. A good strategy is to buy your favorite everyday red and white wines and sparkling water by the case, so you're always ready for company.

Serving a variety of wines at a single meal can make the dinner feel special. Wines are often better appreciated when they progress from white to red, or lighter to heavier, over the course of the meal.

Sparkling wines, which include French Champagne, Italian Prosecco, Spanish cava, and California bottlings, pair nicely with hors d'oeuvres and can be served with a first course or with dessert.

White wines range from light-bodied (Riesling, Pinot Gris, Soave) to medium-bodied (Bordeaux, Sauvignon Blanc, Grüner Veltliner) to full-bodied (Chardonnay). They vary in sweetness, with a crisp, dry Chardonnay or Bordeaux at one end of the spectrum and a fruitier Riesling or Gewürztraminer at the other. Likewise, red

MATCHING FOOD AND WINE

Set aside rules like "red with meat, white with fish." Think about the characteristics of the dish (light, rich, etc.) and choose wines that mirror or contrast those qualities. Here are some helpful hints for pairings.

Appetizers and savory snacks Sparkling wines: *Champagne, Prosecco, cava*

Spicy, salty, or smoked dishes Fruity, light-bodied wines: *Riesling, Gewürztraminer, Grüner Veltliner, rosé, Pinot Gris, Lambrusco, Pinot Noir*

Acidic dishes High-acid wines: *white Bordeaux, Sauvignon Blanc, Zinfandel, Chianti*

Braised, roasted, or grilled beef Full-bodied reds: *Cabernet Sauvignon, Barbaresco, Barolo, Zinfandel, Rioja, Sangiovese, Syrah*

Roasted or grilled chicken and fish Dry whites: *Albariño, Chardonnay, Pinot Grigio, Sancerre, Vermentino, Viognier*

Roasted or grilled lamb Medium-bodied reds: *Burgundy, Côtes du Rhône, Merlot, Pinot Noir, Tempranillo*

Desserts Sweet wines: *Sauternes, vin santo, Muscat, port*

wines also range from light-bodied (Bardolino, Beaujolais, Chianti) to medium-bodied (Merlot, Pinot Noir, Sangiovese, Barbera) to full-bodied (Cabernet Sauvignon, Syrah).

Dessert wines, such as Sauternes, Tocai, and vin santo, are smooth, rich, and sweet, while fortified wines (Madeira, port, sherry) are ideal aperitifs or digestifs.

Serve sparkling wines very cold (42°–45°F/ 6°–7°C), whites cold (50°F/10°C), and reds at cool room temperature. White wines should be chilled for at least 2 hours in the refrigerator or at least 20 minutes in an ice bucket (with equal parts ice and water).

Cocktails Make it Special

A signature mixed drink, whipped up in a cocktail shaker, is always a hit and a great way to personalize a party. You may want to practice making the cocktail before the party, so that everything goes smoothly. Select glassware that will show off the drink, and prepare a garnish that complements whatever spirits you're using, such as a mint sprig, a twist of lemon peel, or chunks of fruit skewered on a cocktail pick.

Bar Basics

Drinks are the stars at a cocktail party, so plan to offer one or two signature cocktails and one nonalcoholic option, along with wine, beer, water, soft drinks, and a well-stocked bar.

When purchasing alcohol and mixers, avoid very large bottles, because once they are opened, their quality deteriorates within a few weeks.

Instead, buy multiple fifths, quarts, liters, and smaller bottles, which, if unopened, will keep indefinitely. Purchase party ice and store it in a cooler or in the freezer, setting some out in an ice bucket on the bar and replenishing it throughout the party. Buy more ice than you think you will need, especially if you plan to chill glasses or bottled drinks. Chill glasses by either filling them with ice (discard before using) or placing in the freezer for 15–30 minutes.

Remember to have plenty of nonalcoholic options on hand. At dinner parties, offer chilled still or sparkling water throughout the meal (lemon slices, mint sprigs, or cucumber disks add a refreshing hit of flavor to the water).

Setting up the Bar

Choose a central location for the bar, in or near the kitchen for easy access to water, ice, and refrigeration. For large parties, set up a full bar for cocktails and mixed drinks and a satellite station for self-serve beverages. Set out garnishes, such as fruit, olives, herb sprigs, citrus twists, swizzle sticks, and decorative picks, in neatly arranged containers on the bar. For outdoor parties, set up a self-serve beverage station in a cool spot. Fill a galvanized tub with ice and pack it with white wine, beer, sodas, juices, and bottles of water. Even for intimate gatherings, setting up a beverage tray in advance makes the party run more smoothly. This can be as simple as putting beverages, ice, glassware, and cocktail napkins in a designated spot.

BAR ESSENTIALS

For a well-outfitted home bar, stock up with the following supplies:

- Mixing glass, jigger or shot glass, and measuring spoons
- Cocktail shaker and strainer
- Bar spoon and muddler; citrus reamer, citrus stripper, and citrus zester
- Ice bucket and tongs; pitchers, decanters, and punch bowl
- Small cutting board and paring knife
- Corkscrew, foil cutter, and bottle opener
- Bar towels, cocktail napkins, and coasters; straws, cocktail picks, swizzle sticks, and decorative charms for wineglass stems
- Blender

BEVERAGE PLANNING

Here are basic guidelines for planning the number of drinks to serve at a typical 2½-hour party. Adjust up or down depending on the weather, age of guests, time of day, and amount of food being served.

Bottled Water Chill 1 large bottle for every 2 guests; have both sparkling and still on hand.

Wine or Sparkling Wine Have on hand 1 bottle for every 2 or 3 wine drinkers, plus a few extra bottles.

Beer Plan on 2 to 3 bottles for every beer drinker; offer at least two different types, light and dark.

Liquor Buy 1 quart (1 l) for every 10 to 12 drinkers (plus mixers, if needed).

Coffee For drip coffee, calculate 1 heaping tablespoon of ground coffee per brewed cup (½ pound/250 g yields about 25 cups).

Tea Calculate 1 teaspoon of loose tea and 1 cup (8 fl oz/250 ml) of boiling water per person, plus 1 extra teaspoon of tea for the pot (¼ pound/125 g yields about 35 cups).

Ice Plan on 1 to 1½ pounds (500 to 750 g) of ice per person, or more if chilling wine and bottled drinks. (If making your own ice, use filtered or bottled water to avoid off flavors.)

spring

drinks and starters

MANGO FIZZ 21

WHITE LILLET COCKTAILS 21

MOJITOS 22

STRAWBERRY DAIQUIRIS 22

APPLE LIMEADE 25

SPARKLING MINT LEMONADE 25

CAMPARI AND ORANGE COCKTAILS 26

PEACH NECTAR SPRITZERS 26

CROSTINI WITH FAVA BEAN SPREAD AND MINT 31

FRIED ARTICHOKES WITH AIOLI 32

SMOKED SALMON AND WATERCRESS WRAPS 35

ENDIVE TIPPED WITH AHI AND GREEN PEPPERCORNS 35

OVEN-ROASTED PESTO SHRIMP SKEWERS 36

ASPARAGUS WITH DIPPING SAUCE 39

RADISHES WITH BUTTER AND SEA SALT 39

MARINATED FETA CUBES 40

BITE-SIZED LEEK TARTLETS 40

soups and salads

CREAMED BROCCOLI-LEEK SOUP 43

SHREDDED CHICKEN SALAD WITH SHERRY DRESSING 44

BABY SPINACH SALAD WITH PARMESAN AND PAPAYA 47

BUTTER LETTUCE AND HERB SALAD WITH
DIJON VINAIGRETTE 47

ARUGULA, FENNEL, AND ORANGE SALAD 48

mains and sides

ROASTED FISH WITH CHIVE BUTTER AND CAVIAR 51

MUSHROOM-STUFFED CHICKEN WITH
SPRING VEGETABLES 52

BONELESS LEG OF LAMB WITH HERBES
DE PROVENCE 55

LEMON RISOTTO 56

FLAGEOLET BEANS WITH OREGANO 59

ROASTED ASPARAGUS 59

CHEDDAR AND CHIVE BISCUITS 60

desserts

STRAWBERRY-RHUBARB GALETTE 63

CHOCOLATE ESPRESSO CRÈMES WITH
CANDIED CITRUS 64

LEMON CUSTARDS WITH LEMON VERBENA CREAM 67

FRUIT COMPOTE WITH BROWN SUGAR COOKIES 68

LEMON POUND CAKE 71

FROZEN TIRAMISU 72

MANGO FIZZ

Select 4 tumblers or highball glasses. Fill each glass with ice. Add 6 tablespoons (3 fl oz/90 ml) of the mango nectar, ¼ cup (2 fl oz/60 ml) of the orange juice, and 2 tablespoons of the lime juice to each glass and stir. Top with ¼ cup (2 fl oz/60 ml) sparkling water. Stir, garnish each glass with a mango wedge, and serve at once.

Ice cubes or crushed ice

1½ cups (12 fl oz/375 ml) mango nectar

1 cup (8 fl oz/250 ml) fresh orange juice

½ cup (4 fl oz/125 ml) fresh lime juice (3–4 limes)

1 cup (8 fl oz/250 ml) sparkling water, chilled

4 mango wedges for garnish

SERVES 4

WHITE LILLET COCKTAILS

Select 4 tumblers or highball glasses. Fill each glass with ice. Add about ¾ cup (6 fl oz/180 ml) of the Lillet and 1 tablespoon of the Cointreau to each glass and stir. Garnish each glass with an orange peel strip and serve at once.

Ice cubes

1 bottle (24 fl oz/750 ml) white Lillet

¼ cup (2 fl oz/60 ml) Cointreau

4 orange peel strips, each about ¼ inch (6 mm) wide and 4 inches (10 cm) long, for garnish

SERVES 4

MOJITOS

Select 4 tall or highball glasses. Put 8 of the mint sprigs, 1 tablespoon of the sugar, and the juice of 1 lime in each glass. Muddle to bruise, but not pulverize, the mint. Add some ice and ¼ cup (2 fl oz/ 60 ml) of the rum to each glass. Top each glass with sparkling water, stir well, and serve at once.

32 fresh mint sprigs

4 tablespoons (1¾ oz/50 g) superfine (caster) sugar

Juice of 4 limes

Ice cubes

1 cup (8 fl oz/250 ml) light rum

1 bottle (24 fl oz/750 ml) sparkling water

SERVES 4

STRAWBERRY DAIQUIRIS

Select 4 cocktail glasses. In a blender, combine the strawberry purée, rum, sugar, and lime juice. Add ice to cover by 1½ inches (4 cm) and process until liquefied. Pour into the glasses and garnish each glass with a strawberry half, resting it on the rim. Serve at once.

¾ cup (6 fl oz/ 180 ml) puréed sweetened frozen strawberries

1 cup (8 fl oz/250 ml) light rum

4 teaspoons sugar

Juice of 4 limes

Ice cubes

2 strawberries with hulls intact, halved lengthwise, for garnish

SERVES 4

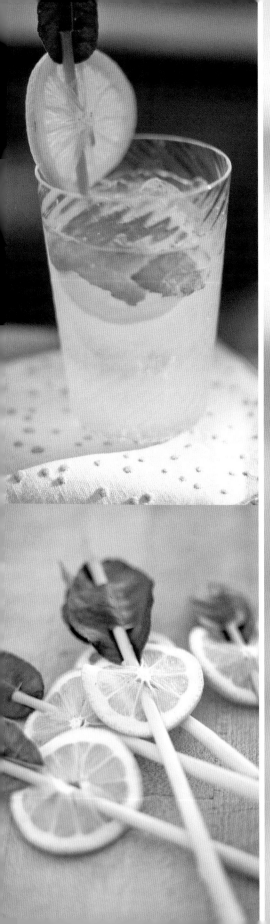

APPLE LIMEADE

To vary this quick and easy drink, add ½ cup (½ oz/15 g) fresh mint leaves or 1 tablespoon peeled and finely grated fresh ginger to the juice mixture before refrigerating. Seek out unfiltered apple juice, also sold as sweet apple cider, for its intense apple flavor.

Cut 10 of the limes in half and juice them. You should have about 1 cup (8 fl oz/250 ml) juice. Reserve 6 squeezed lime halves and discard the rest. In a large glass jar or pitcher, stir together the lime juice, apple juice, and the reserved lime halves. Cover and refrigerate for at least 1 hour or up to 12 hours to blend the flavors.

When ready to serve, cut the remaining 2 limes into 6 slices each. Fill a large serving pitcher half full with ice and add the sparkling water, lime slices, and apple slices. Strain the apple juice mixture through a fine-mesh sieve into the pitcher and stir. Pour into tall chilled glasses over ice and serve at once.

12 limes

4 cups (32 fl oz/1 l) unfiltered apple juice

Ice cubes

1 bottle (24 fl oz/750 ml) sparkling water

2 small Granny Smith apples, halved, cored, and sliced

SERVES 6

SPARKLING MINT LEMONADE

Lemonade is a welcome drink when springtime temperatures start to rise. Choose lemons that are plump and firm. Before juicing each lemon, press and roll it firmly against a work surface to break some of the membranes holding the juice.

In a saucepan over medium heat, combine the sugar with 2 cups (16 fl oz/500 ml) water and the lemon peel. Bring to a boil, stirring to dissolve the sugar, and boil for 1 minute. Remove from the heat, stir in the 4 large mint sprigs, and let stand for 30 minutes to infuse the syrup with the mint. Discard the mint sprigs. Strain the syrup through a fine-mesh sieve into a small pitcher or bowl. Stir in the lemon juice and refrigerate until cold.

Just before serving, transfer the syrup mixture to 1 or 2 pitchers or a large punch bowl, add the sparkling water, and stir well. Add ice cubes. Serve in tumblers and garnish each serving with a lemon slice and a mint sprig.

2 cups (1 lb/500 g) sugar

4 lemon peel strips, each 3 inches (7.5 cm) long, plus 12 lemon slices for garnish

4 large fresh mint sprigs, plus 12 small sprigs for garnish

1½ cups (12 fl oz/375 ml) fresh lemon juice (8–10 lemons)

3 bottles (24 fl oz/750 ml each) sparkling water, chilled

Ice cubes

SERVES 12

CAMPARI AND ORANGE COCKTAILS

Put 4 old-fashioned glasses or other short, stocky glasses in the freezer to chill for at least 15 minutes. Just before serving, fill a cocktail shaker half full with crushed ice. Pour in half each of the orange juice, Campari, Grand Marnier, and vodka. Cover with the lid and shake vigorously for about 10 seconds. Strain into 2 of the chilled glasses. Repeat with the remaining cocktail ingredients and glasses to make 2 more drinks. Garnish each glass with an orange slice and serve at once.

Crushed ice

1 cup (8 fl oz/250 ml) fresh orange juice

¼ cup (2 fl oz/60 ml) Campari

¼ cup (2 fl oz/60 ml) Grand Marnier or other orange liqueur

¼ cup (2 fl oz/60 ml) vodka or gin

4 orange slices

SERVES 4

PEACH NECTAR SPRITZERS

Fill 6 tall glasses half full with ice cubes. Pour ½ cup (4 fl oz/125 ml) of the peach nectar into each glass and fill with the sparkling water. (Alternatively, fill a pitcher half full with ice cubes, pour both cans of peach nectar into the pitcher, and stir in the sparkling water.)

Garnish each glass with a few peach slices. Serve at once.

Ice cubes

2 cans (12 fl oz/375 ml each) peach nectar

1 bottle (24 fl oz/750 ml) sparkling mineral water

1 peach, halved, pitted, and thinly sliced

SERVES 6

CROSTINI WITH FAVA BEAN SPREAD AND MINT

Fresh fava beans are prized for their meaty, earthy taste, not dissimilar to that of lima beans. The larger, more mature beans make an exceptional spread and combine well with fresh herbs. Here, fresh mint is used, but chives or tarragon can be used in its place.

Preheat the oven to 350°F (180°C).

Arrange the baguette slices in a single layer on a baking sheet. Bake, turning once halfway through baking, until lightly golden, about 20 minutes. Remove from the oven and set aside.

Remove the fava beans from their pods and discard the pods. Bring a pot three-fourths full of water to a boil over high heat. Add the fava beans and cook until the beans are tender and the skins slip easily from the beans, 10–25 minutes; the timing depends on the age of the beans. Drain the beans in a colander and, when cool enough to handle, slip off the skins and discard them.

In a food processor or blender, combine the beans, the 3 tablespoons olive oil, 3 tablespoons of the cream, the salt, the pepper, and the minced mint and process until a creamy purée forms. If the mixture seems too dry, add up to 3 tablespoons more cream. Taste and adjust the seasoning. (The purée may be made up to 2 hours in advance, covered, and refrigerated; bring to room temperature before spreading on the baguette slices.)

Spread the purée on the baguette slices and arrange on a platter. Garnish the crostini with the mint sprigs and then drizzle them with olive oil. Serve at once.

30 baguette slices, ¼ inch (6 mm) thick (about 1 large baguette)

2 lb (1 kg) fava (broad) beans

3 tablespoons extra-virgin olive oil, plus extra for drizzling

6 tablespoons (3 fl oz/90 ml) heavy (double) cream

2 teaspoons sea salt

1 teaspoon freshly ground pepper

3 tablespoons minced fresh mint

30 small fresh mint sprigs for garnish

SERVES 10–12

FRIED ARTICHOKES WITH AIOLI

Thinly sliced artichokes turn golden and crisp when fried, perfect for eating out of hand. Artichokes begin to discolor when cut, so drop them into lemon water after slicing them, making sure to pat the slices dry before adding them to hot oil. If you make the aioli in advance, keep in mind that the flavor intensifies over time.

To make the aioli, put the salt and garlic in a mortar or small bowl. Using a pestle or the back of a wooden spoon, crush together the salt and garlic to make a coarse paste. Transfer the paste to a large bowl. Using a whisk, beat in the egg yolks. Very slowly drizzle in ½ cup (4 fl oz/ 125 ml) of the olive oil while continuing to beat until blended and the mixture starts to stiffen. Do not add too much at once or the mixture will not hold together. Once the mixture has begun to stiffen, drizzle in ¼–½ cup (2–4 fl oz/ 60–125 ml) of the remaining olive oil while continuing to beat, stopping when the mixture is quite stiff. Transfer to a serving bowl, cover, and refrigerate until ready to serve. (The aioli can be made up to 1 day in advance.)

To prepare the artichokes, fill a large bowl halfway with cold water and add the lemon juice. Working with 1 artichoke at a time, break off about 3 layers of the dark green outer leaves until you reach the pale golden yellow inner leaves. If the inner leaves have any purple coloring or are prickly, remove them. Cut off the top one-fourth of the leaves, and then trim off the stem. Using a knife or mandoline, cut each artichoke lengthwise into slices ¼ inch (6 mm) thick, and immediately drop the slices into the lemon water.

In a frying pan over medium-high heat, warm the olive oil. When the oil is hot, drain the artichoke slices and pat dry. Working in batches, fry the artichoke slices, turning several times, until crisp and golden, 3–4 minutes. Using a slotted spoon, transfer to paper towels to drain. When all the artichokes are fried, sprinkle with the salt. (The artichokes may be fried up to 2 hours in advance, but don't add the salt until just before serving.)

Transfer the artichokes to a platter and garnish with the lemon wedges. Serve at room temperature with the aioli.

Aioli

½ teaspoon sea salt

2 cloves garlic, coarsely chopped

2 large egg yolks

1 cup (8 fl oz/250 ml) extra-virgin olive oil

Artichokes

3 tablespoons fresh lemon juice

12–16 baby artichokes

¼ cup (2 fl oz/60 ml) extra-virgin olive oil

1 teaspoon sea salt

Lemon wedges for garnish

SERVES 6–8

SMOKED SALMON AND WATERCRESS WRAPS

In a bowl, mix together the goat cheese and half-and-half until the mixture has a smooth, spreadable consistency. Spread each tortilla with one-third of the cheese mixture, covering the entire surface. Place one-third of the salmon strips on top of the cheese and top with one-third of the watercress leaves. Roll up each tortilla into a snug cylinder and place, seam side down, on a cutting board. Using a serrated knife, cut crosswise into slices about 1 inch (2.5 cm) wide. Arrange the slices on a platter, garnish with the watercress sprigs, and serve.

3 oz (90 g) herbed fresh goat cheese, at room temperature

3 tablespoons half-and-half (half cream)

3 large flour tortillas

5 oz (155 g) sliced smoked salmon, cut into strips 1 inch (2.5 cm) wide

Leaves from 2 bunches watercress, tough stems removed (about 1 cup/ 1 oz/30 g leaves), plus sprigs for garnish

SERVES 12–14

ENDIVE TIPPED WITH AHI AND GREEN PEPPERCORNS

Cut off ½ inch (12 mm) from the stem end of each endive. Separate the leaves, then choose the 40 largest leaves (reserve the others for another use). Spread about 1½ teaspoons of cream cheese at the base end of each leaf, covering one-fourth of the leaf. Sprinkle with about 1 teaspoon tuna and a few of the peppercorns. Cover and refrigerate until serving. They will keep for up to 4 hours.

5 heads Belgian endive (chicory/witloof)

1 package (8 oz/250 g) cream cheese, at room temperature

1 lb (500 g) sashimi-grade ahi tuna, finely diced

⅓ cup (2½ oz/75 g) pickled green peppercorns, rinsed and patted dry

SERVES 12–14

OVEN-ROASTED PESTO SHRIMP SKEWERS

Position a rack in the upper third of the oven and preheat to 400°F (200°C). Line a large baking sheet with parchment (baking) paper. Soak 30 small wooden skewers in water to cover for 10 minutes and then drain.

In a bowl, combine the shrimp and pesto and toss until the shrimp are evenly coated. Thread 2 shrimp onto each skewer. (The skewers can be prepared up to this point, covered with plastic wrap, and refrigerated for up to 24 hours.)

Arrange the skewers in a single layer on the prepared baking sheet. Sprinkle with the red pepper flakes. Roast the shrimp until just opaque throughout, 8–10 minutes. Transfer the shrimp skewers to a warmed platter. Serve at once.

1 package (2 lb/1 kg) frozen uncooked peeled and deveined medium shrimp (prawns), about 60 total, thawed

1 container (7 oz/220 g) prepared pesto

1/2 teaspoon red pepper flakes

MAKES 30 SKEWERS; SERVES 12

ASPARAGUS WITH DIPPING SAUCE

Preheat the oven to 450°F (230°C).

Arrange the asparagus spears in a single layer in
2 shallow baking dishes. Drizzle with the vinegar
and olive oil, then sprinkle with the salt and
pepper. Turn several times to coat the spears well.
Roast, turning several times, until tender but crisp
and the tips are lightly golden, 10–15 minutes.
Transfer to a platter.

To make the dipping sauce, in a small bowl, whisk
together the cheese, olive oil, yogurt, and parsley.
Whisk in salt and pepper to taste.

Transfer the sauce to a serving bowl and place
alongside the platter of asparagus. Serve at
room temperature.

48 asparagus spears,
ends trimmed

1/3 cup (3 fl oz/90 ml)
balsamic vinegar

1/4 cup (2 fl oz/60 ml)
extra-virgin olive oil

1 teaspoon salt

1 teaspoon freshly
ground pepper

Dipping Sauce

1/4 lb (125 g) freshly
grated Parmesan cheese

2 tablespoons
extra-virgin olive oil

1/4 cup (2 oz/60 g)
plain yogurt

2 tablespoons
minced fresh flat-leaf
(Italian) parsley

Salt and freshly
ground pepper

SERVES 12–14

RADISHES WITH BUTTER AND SEA SALT

Trim the thin roots from the radishes but don't cut
into the body. Remove all but a few of the youngest,
smallest leaves from the tops. Cut each radish in half.

Put the butter into a ramekin just large enough to
hold it, and smooth the top with a knife. Put the
sea salt in a small dish.

To serve, arrange the radish halves on a platter with
the butter and salt and several small butter knives.

2 bunches radishes
with leaves attached
(18–20 radishes)

1/2 cup (4 oz/125 g)
unsalted butter, at
room temperature

3 tablespoons sea salt

SERVES 8–10

MARINATED FETA CUBES

The tangy, salty flavor of feta cheese is a perfect match for cocktails. Buy jars of precut feta cubes packed in olive oil with herbs and garlic. Mini marinated mozzarella balls are also readily available and can be served alongside, or in place of, the feta cubes.

Drain the feta cubes in a colander. To serve, transfer the feta to a plate or shallow serving bowl. Drizzle the feta cubes with olive oil. Place a toothpick in each cube, or fill a shot glass with toothpicks and place it in the center of the bowl with the feta cubes arranged around it. Include an empty bowl alongside, so that guests can discard the used toothpicks; place a toothpick in the bowl to indicate its use.

2 jars (10½ oz/330 g each) marinated feta cheese cubes

Extra-virgin olive oil for drizzling

SERVES 12

BITE-SIZED LEEK TARTLETS

Use the ready-to-roll-out pastry dough available at supermarkets to make the pastry shells for these savory treats. They can be baked up to 12 hours in advance and stored at room temperature in an airtight container or resealable plastic bag.

Preheat the oven to 400°F (200°C). Have ready mini-muffin pans with 24 cups. Using a 2-inch (5-cm) round cookie cutter, cut out 24 pastry rounds, reserving any extra dough. Fit a round into each muffin cup. To keep the pastry flat while baking, make a loose ball of aluminum foil and place into each cup. Bake for 4 minutes. Remove the foil, prick each pastry shell with fork tines, and bake for 2–3 minutes longer. Repeat with the remaining dough. Let cool on wire racks. Reduce the oven temperature to 350°F (180°C).

In a frying pan over medium heat, melt the butter. Add the leek and cook, stirring, until softened, about 15 minutes. Cover, reduce the heat to low, and cook until translucent, 5–7 minutes longer. Set aside.

In a bowl, whisk together the eggs, cream, salt, pepper, and nutmeg. Whisk in the leek mixture, then spoon into the cooled pastry shells, filling to the brim. Bake until puffed and lightly golden, 10–12 minutes. Let cool in the pans on a wire rack. Serve warm or at room temperature.

3 rolls store-bought pie pastry dough, each about 13 inches (33 cm) in diameter and ¼ inch (6 mm) thick, thawed in the refrigerator

2 tablespoons unsalted butter

1 large leek, white part only, minced

3 large eggs, at room temperature

1¾ cups (14 fl oz/430 ml) heavy (double) cream or half-and-half (half cream)

½ teaspoon salt

¼ teaspoon ground white pepper

⅛ teaspoon freshly grated nutmeg

SERVES 12–14

CREAMED BROCCOLI-LEEK SOUP

Leeks and broccoli are at their best in the springtime, when they are still tender and at the height of their flavor. If you can, use homemade vegetable or chicken stock—it will deliver a richer flavor than purchased broth. For a tangier finish to this smooth and creamy soup, use crumbled goat cheese in place of the blue cheese garnish.

In a large saucepan over medium-high heat, warm the olive oil. Add the garlic, broccoli, leek, and mustard and sauté until the leek is soft and translucent and the broccoli is bright green, about 5 minutes. Add the oregano and broth and bring to a boil. Reduce the heat to low, cover partially, and simmer until the broccoli is tender, about 20 minutes.

Remove from the heat and process with an immersion blender or food processor until smooth. Stir in the cream and season to taste with salt and pepper. (The soup can be prepared up to this point, cooled, covered, and refrigerated for up to 24 hours. When ready to serve, reheat gently over medium-low heat, thinning the soup with more broth if needed.)

Ladle into warmed bowls and top each serving with a little blue cheese and a sprinkle of oregano leaves. Serve at once.

Homemade croutons

Serve this soup garnished with large, crunchy croutons. To make your own, arrange thin baguette slices on a rimmed baking sheet and brush lightly on both sides with olive oil. Bake in a preheated 350°F (180°C) oven, turning once, until lightly browned, 8–10 minutes on each side.

3 tablespoons olive oil

2 cloves garlic

1 package (12 oz/375 g) precut broccoli crowns or florets

1 leek, including tender, pale green part, finely chopped

1 tablespoon coarse-grain mustard

2 tablespoons fresh oregano leaves, plus a few leaves for garnish

4 cups (32 fl oz/1 l) vegetable or low-sodium chicken broth

1/4 cup (2 fl oz/60 ml) heavy (double) cream

Coarse salt and freshly ground pepper

Crumbled blue cheese for garnish

SERVES 4

SHREDDED CHICKEN SALAD WITH SHERRY DRESSING

Versatile time-savers, rotisserie chickens are readily available at most supermarkets. Here, shreds of roasted chicken partner with tender spring onions and watercress greens in a seasonal salad. If you can find fresh English peas, which begin to appear in markets in early spring, use them in place of the frozen peas (shell them first and then blanch them according to the recipe directions).

To make the dressing, in a food processor, combine the mayonnaise, sour cream, sherry, soy sauce, and green onions. Purée until smooth and emulsified. Season to taste with salt and pepper. Transfer to a small bowl, cover, and refrigerate until ready to serve. (The dressing can be prepared in advance and refrigerated for up to 24 hours.)

Bring a small saucepan half full of water to a boil, add the peas, and blanch for 30 seconds. Drain the peas and refresh them under running cold water. Set aside to let drain completely.

Remove the skin from the roasted chicken and discard. Using your fingers, pull the meat from the bones and shred it into bite-sized pieces.

In a large bowl, combine the chicken meat, celery, watercress, walnut pieces, and peas. Add the dressing and toss to coat the salad evenly. To serve, divide the salad among chilled individual plates. Serve at once.

Make it a meal

This hearty salad can be served as a main dish alongside a bowl of soup (such as Creamed Broccoli-Leek Soup, page 43). Or, transform it into a sandwich for your next picnic lunch—simply omit the walnuts and spoon the salad between slices of French or sourdough bread.

Dressing

½ cup (4 fl oz/125 ml) mayonnaise

¼ cup (2 oz/60 g) sour cream

3 tablespoons dry sherry

1 tablespoon soy sauce

2 green (spring) onions, including tender green tops, chopped

Coarse salt and freshly ground pepper

1 cup (5 oz/155 g) frozen petite peas

1 roasted chicken, about 4 lb (2 kg)

1 celery stalk, thinly sliced

1 bunch young, tender watercress, tough stems removed

⅓ cup (1½ oz/45 g) walnut pieces

SERVES 4

BABY SPINACH SALAD WITH PARMESAN AND PAPAYA

Using a vegetable peeler, shave the cheese into thin ribbons. Set aside. Peel and seed the papayas, then cut them into 1/2-inch (12-mm) cubes.

In a large salad bowl, combine the olive oil, vinegars, salt, and ground peppercorns and mix well with a fork or whisk. Add the spinach and toss well to coat. Add the papayas and half of the Parmesan, and turn gently to coat. Top with the remaining Parmesan and garnish with more ground peppercorns. Serve at once.

4 oz (125 g) Parmesan cheese

4 ripe papayas

1/4 cup (2 fl oz/60 ml) extra-virgin olive oil

1 tablespoon white balsamic vinegar

2 teaspoons red wine vinegar

1/2 teaspoon sea salt

1 1/2 teaspoons freshly ground pink peppercorns, plus extra for garnish

10 cups (10 oz/315 g) baby spinach

SERVES 10–12

BUTTER LETTUCE AND HERB SALAD WITH DIJON VINAIGRETTE

Carefully separate the lettuce leaves. Tear only the largest outer leaves into halves and leave the remaining leaves whole.

In a large salad bowl, combine the olive oil, vinegar, mustard, salt, and pepper and mix well with a fork or whisk. Add the lettuce, chopped parsley, and parsley leaves and toss gently to coat. Serve at once.

2 heads butter lettuce

3 1/2 tablespoons extra-virgin olive oil

1 1/2 tablespoons red wine vinegar

2 teaspoons Dijon mustard

1/2 teaspoon sea salt

1/2 teaspoon freshly ground pepper

1/3 cup (1/2 oz/15 g) finely chopped fresh flat-leaf (Italian) parsley, plus 1/2 cup (1/2 oz/15 g) leaves

SERVES 6–8

ARUGULA, FENNEL, AND ORANGE SALAD

To make the vinaigrette, in a small bowl, whisk together the orange juice, lemon juice, orange zest, olive oil, canola oil, mustard, tarragon, and shallot. Season to taste with salt and pepper. Set aside.

Cut off the stems and feathery fronds of the fennel bulb and remove any bruised or discolored outer layers. Cut the bulb in half lengthwise and cut out any tough core parts. Cut the bulb halves crosswise into slices ⅜ inch (1 cm) thick, and then cut the slices into 1-inch (2.5-cm) lengths.

Working with 1 orange at a time, and using a sharp knife, cut a slice off both ends of the orange to reveal the flesh. Stand the orange upright on a cutting board and thickly slice off the peel and pith in strips, following the contour of the fruit. Cut the orange in half crosswise, place each half cut side down, and thinly slice vertically to create half-moons. Repeat with the remaining oranges.

Place the fennel and arugula in a large serving bowl, add half of the vinaigrette, and toss gently to coat thoroughly. Arrange the orange slices in a pinwheel or other design on top. Drizzle with the remaining vinaigrette and serve.

Citrus Vinaigrette

¼ cup (2 fl oz/60 ml) fresh orange juice

2 tablespoons fresh lemon juice

2 teaspoons grated orange zest

2 tablespoons extra-virgin olive oil

2 tablespoons canola oil

2 teaspoons Dijon mustard

½ teaspoon dried tarragon

1 shallot, chopped

Salt and freshly ground pepper

1 large fennel bulb

3 large navel oranges

4 cups (4 oz/125 g) arugula (rocket)

SERVES 8–10

ROASTED FISH WITH CHIVE BUTTER AND CAVIAR

Any type of firm white fish, such as halibut, cod, or sea bass, can be used here. When buying fish, ask for fillets that are uniform in size and weight to ensure even cooking. The chive butter is easy to make and versatile—try it on baked potatoes or grilled steak, or spread it on warm bread.

To make the chive butter, in a food processor, combine the butter, chopped chives, lemon juice, and ¼ teaspoon pepper and pulse until the chives are evenly distributed throughout the butter. Using a rubber spatula, scrape the chive butter onto a piece of plastic wrap and form into a log. Refrigerate for at least 30 minutes or up to 24 hours.

Preheat the oven to 450°F (230°C). Pat the halibut fillets dry with paper towels and place the fillets on a nonstick rimmed baking sheet. Brush the fillets with the olive oil and season with salt and pepper. Roast the fillets until they start to turn golden and are just opaque at the center when tested with a knife, about 8 minutes.

While the fish is roasting, remove the chive butter from the refrigerator and cut the log into 6 equal pieces. Set aside.

To serve, place 1 halibut fillet in the center of each warmed individual plate and top with a pat of the chive butter. Spoon a dollop of the caviar onto each serving and garnish with a sprinkle of chives. Serve at once.

Serving suggestions

Serve this elegant springtime dish with a simple salad of mixed baby greens tossed with fresh lemon juice and olive oil and a side of roasted asparagus or new potatoes. A crisp white wine, such as Sauvignon Blanc or Pinot Grigio, is a good match for this dish.

Chive Butter

½ cup (4 oz/125 g) unsalted butter, at room temperature

¼ cup (½ oz/15 g) chopped fresh chives

1 tablespoon fresh lemon juice

¼ teaspoon freshly ground pepper

6 halibut or other firm, white fish fillets, each 6 oz (185 g) and about 1½ inches (4 cm) thick

3 tablespoons olive oil

Coarse salt and freshly ground pepper

1 oz (30 g) osetra or sevruga caviar or American paddlefish roe

10 fresh chives, cut into 2-inch (5-cm) lengths

SERVES 6

MUSHROOM-STUFFED CHICKEN WITH SPRING VEGETABLES

Plentiful in the spring, baby vegetables are more tender and flavorful than mature ones. If they aren't available, you can use larger vegetables, but parboil them before adding them to the roasting pan. Rubbing the chicken with butter before roasting it ensures a crisp, golden skin.

Preheat the oven to 400°F (200°C). Spread the bread cubes on a baking sheet and toast, turning once, until golden brown, about 15 minutes. Set aside. (The bread cubes can be toasted up to 3 weeks in advance and stored in an airtight container.) Reduce the oven temperature to 350°F (180°C). Select a roasting pan just large enough to accommodate the 2 chickens and place a rack in the pan.

Finely chop the chicken giblets and set aside. In a frying pan over medium heat, melt 4 tablespoons (2 oz/60 g) of the butter. Add half of the mushrooms, the shallots, 1/2 teaspoon each of the salt and pepper, and the thyme. Cook, stirring, until the mushrooms are tender, 4–5 minutes. Add 1/2 cup (4 fl oz/125 ml) of the stock and transfer to a bowl. Stir in the bread cubes, parsley, and chopped giblets.

Rub each chicken inside and out with the remaining 2 tablespoons butter. Season with the remaining 1/2 teaspoon each salt and pepper. Pack the cavities snugly with the stuffing and truss the legs with string. Place on the rack and roast for 30 minutes. Remove the chickens from the oven and discard the string. Place the

onions, carrots, and potatoes around the chickens and turn to coat with the pan juices. Roast until an instant-read thermometer inserted into the thickest part of the thigh away from the bone registers 170°F (77°C) and the vegetables are tender, about 1 hour longer. Transfer the vegetables and chickens to 1 or 2 platters, and tent with aluminum foil.

Discard all but 2 tablespoons of the juices from the roasting pan, place over medium heat, add the remaining mushrooms, and cook just until softened, 2–3 minutes. Using a slotted spoon, transfer the mushrooms to a bowl. Turn off the heat. Add the brandy and 1/4 cup (2 fl oz/65 ml) stock, scraping up any browned bits on the pan bottom. Return the heat to medium-high, add the remaining 3/4 cup (6 fl oz/180 ml) stock, and cook, stirring, until the sauce is reduced and thickened, 1–2 minutes. Stir in the mushrooms, remove from the heat, and cover to keep warm.

Remove the stuffing and carve the chickens. To serve, arrange a piece of chicken on each plate, surround with the stuffing and vegetables, and top with the sauce.

6–8 baguette slices, 1 inch (2.5 cm) thick, cut into 1-inch cubes

2 chickens, about 4 lb (2 kg) each, with giblets

6 tablespoons (3 oz/90 g) unsalted butter

1 lb (500 g) mixed fresh mushrooms such as chanterelle, porcini, oyster, and portobello, halved or quartered

1/4 cup (1 1/2 oz/45 g) minced shallots

1 teaspoon each salt and freshly ground pepper

2 teaspoons minced fresh thyme

1 1/2 cups (12 fl oz/375 ml) chicken stock or reduced-sodium chicken broth

2 tablespoons minced fresh flat-leaf (Italian) parsley

12–14 green (spring) onions, trimmed and halved lengthwise

8–10 young carrots, trimmed and halved lengthwise

14–16 baby Yukon gold, Red Rose, or White Rose potatoes, halved

1 1/2 tablespoons brandy

SERVES 10–12

BONELESS LEG OF LAMB WITH HERBES DE PROVENCE

Generously studded with garlic and rubbed with a blend of dried herbs characteristic of the south of France, a leg of lamb is often the centerpiece of a Provençal dinner party. Spring is the best time to enjoy fresh, local lamb, when the milk-fed meat is especially young and tender. When purchasing it, look for meat that is pale pink and marbled with very little fat.

Preheat the oven to 400°F (200°C). Select a shallow roasting pan just large enough to accommodate the lamb.

Open up the leg of lamb. In a small bowl, stir together the olive oil, salt, pepper, and herbes de Provence. Rub the herb mixture all over the meat. Roll the lamb back to its original shape. Tie at regular intervals with 3 or 4 lengths of kitchen string. Tie another length of string lengthwise around the rolled lamb. Using a sharp knife, make 20–25 deep slits in the meat, spacing them regularly. Insert a garlic sliver in each slit. (The lamb can be prepared up to 6 hours in advance and refrigerated. Bring to room temperature before roasting.)

Place the lamb in the pan and roast for 15 minutes. Reduce the oven temperature to 350°F (180°C) and continue to roast until an instant-read thermometer inserted into the thickest part of the lamb registers 125°F (52°C) for rare, about 30 minutes longer, or 130°–140°F (54°–60°C) for medium, 35–40 minutes longer. Remove from the oven and transfer the lamb to a cutting board. Tent with aluminum foil and let rest for at least 15 minutes.

Cut the strings from the lamb and discard. Carefully cut the lamb into slices ½ inch (12 mm) thick. Arrange on a warmed serving platter, garnish with the rosemary sprigs, and serve at once.

1 boneless leg of lamb, 3½–4 lb (1.75–2 kg), trimmed of excess fat

2 tablespoons extra-virgin olive oil

1½ teaspoons sea salt

1 teaspoon freshly ground pepper

3 tablespoons herbes de Provence

5 cloves garlic, cut lengthwise into thin slivers

Fresh rosemary sprigs for garnish

SERVES 6–8

LEMON RISOTTO

Early spring brings plenty of citrus and tender herbs to gardens and farmers' markets. This mild, creamy risotto, spiked with lemon zest and a sprinkling of chervil, is especially good served alongside fish or roasted chicken. Be sure to add the lemon zest at the end, so its flavor will be fresh and bright; its volatile oils will quickly dissipate if warmed too long.

In a saucepan over high heat, combine the chicken stock and 3½ cups (28 fl oz/875 ml) water and bring to a boil. Reduce the heat to low and maintain a simmer.

In another saucepan over medium heat, melt 2 tablespoons of the butter with the olive oil. Add the shallots and sauté until translucent, 2–3 minutes. Add the rice and stir until it is opaque, about 3 minutes. Add about ¾ cup (6 fl oz/180 ml) of the simmering stock, adjust the heat to maintain a simmer, and cook, stirring, until most of the stock is absorbed, about 3 minutes. Continue adding the stock, ¾ cup at a time, and stirring constantly, until all but about ½ cup (4 fl oz/125 ml) of the stock has been used, the rice is nearly tender and still slightly firm in the center, and the mixture is creamy, 20–25 minutes.

Add the lemon juice to the remaining ½ cup stock and add the mixture, little by little, to the rice along with the remaining 3 tablespoons butter, the lemon zest, and the grated Parmesan, always stirring constantly. Taste for salt and add as needed.

If desired, stir in the chervil. Transfer to a serving bowl, garnish with shavings of Parmesan, and serve at once.

3 cups (24 fl oz/750 ml) chicken stock or reduced-sodium chicken broth

5 tablespoons (2½ oz/75 g) unsalted butter

3 tablespoons extra-virgin olive oil

3 tablespoons minced shallots

2¼ cups (1 lb/500 g) Arborio rice

½ cup (4 fl oz/125 ml) fresh lemon juice

¼ cup (⅓ oz/10 g) coarsely grated lemon zest

¾ cup (3 oz/90 g) freshly grated Parmesan cheese, plus shaved cheese for garnish

Salt

¼ cup (⅓ oz/10 g) minced fresh chervil (optional)

SERVES 6

FLAGEOLET BEANS WITH OREGANO

Rinse the beans well in a colander, discarding any misshapen beans or stones. In a large saucepan, combine the beans with 2½ quarts (2.5 l) water, 1 teaspoon of the salt, the bay leaves, and the dried oregano and bring to a boil over high heat. Reduce the heat to low, cover, and simmer until the beans are tender to the bite, 1½–2 hours. (The beans can be partially prepared up to 1 day in advance. Remove them from the heat just before they are tender, about 1–1½ hours. The next day, add a little more water and cook, covered, for 20–30 minutes over medium heat until tender.)

Using a slotted spoon, transfer the beans to a bowl. Discard the bay leaves. Stir in the remaining ½ teaspoon salt, the oregano, pepper, and olive oil. Serve hot.

1½ cups (10 oz/315 g) dried flageolet beans

1½ teaspoons salt

2 bay leaves

½ teaspoon dried oregano

1 tablespoon chopped fresh oregano

½ teaspoon freshly ground pepper

2 tablespoons extra-virgin olive oil

SERVES 6–8

ROASTED ASPARAGUS

Preheat the oven to 450°F (230°C). Place the asparagus on a rimmed baking sheet large enough to hold them in a single layer. In a small bowl, using a fork, combine the butter and lemon zest. With your hands, rub the asparagus with the lemon butter until evenly coated. Season with salt and pepper. Roast until lightly browned but still crisp, about 10 minutes. To serve, place a few asparagus on each individual plate and drizzle any pan juices over the top. Serve at once.

1½ lb (750 g) thin asparagus spears, tough ends removed

¼ cup (2 oz/60 g) unsalted butter, at room temperature

1 tablespoon grated lemon zest

Coarse salt and freshly ground pepper

SERVES 6

CHEDDAR AND CHIVE BISCUITS

Minced chives and shreds of white Cheddar cheese lace these flaky biscuits. The dough is easy to mix by hand or using a stand mixer. To make it with buttermilk instead of milk, decrease the baking powder to 2 teaspoons and add ½ teaspoon baking soda (bicarbonate of soda).

Preheat the oven to 425°F (220°C). Lightly butter a rimmed baking sheet.

To make the dough by hand, in a large bowl, stir together the flour, baking powder, salt, cheese, and chives. Using a pastry blender or 2 knives, cut the butter into the flour mixture until it resembles coarse crumbs. Pour in the milk and mix with a fork or rubber spatula just until the dry ingredients are evenly moistened. Transfer the dough to a lightly floured work surface and knead gently a few times until the dough clings together.

To make the dough in a stand mixer, combine the flour, baking powder, salt, cheese, and chives in the mixer bowl. Fit the mixer with the paddle attachment and mix on low speed for a few seconds to combine. Add the butter and mix on medium-low speed just until the mixture forms coarse crumbs. Add the milk and mix for a few seconds until evenly moistened. Transfer the dough to a lightly floured work surface and knead gently a few times until the dough clings together.

Roll or pat out the dough about ½ inch (12 mm) thick. Using a 2-inch (5-cm) biscuit cutter or glass dipped in flour, cut out rounds by pressing straight down and lifting straight up. Do not twist the cutter or glass or the biscuits may become lopsided. Alternatively, roll or pat out the dough into a rectangle and cut into 2-inch (5-cm) squares. Place the biscuits 1 inch (2.5 cm) apart on the prepared baking sheet.

Bake until golden on the edges, 15–18 minutes. Remove from the oven, transfer to a wire rack, and let cool for 10 minutes. Serve warm.

2 cups (10 oz/315 g) all-purpose (plain) flour

2½ teaspoons baking powder

½ teaspoon salt

¾ cup (3 oz/90 g) shredded white Cheddar cheese

⅓ cup (½ oz/15 g) minced fresh chives

6 tablespoons (3 oz/90 g) cold unsalted butter, cut into chunks

¾ cup (6 fl oz/180 ml) whole milk

MAKES ABOUT 18 BISCUITS; SERVES 8–10

STRAWBERRY-RHUBARB GALETTE

Strawberries and rhubarb are a classic springtime combination. This galette, a rustic tart that shows off the fruit in the center, can be served with a small scoop of ice cream, with a dollop of crème fraîche or whipped cream, or on its own, with just a dusting of confectioners' sugar.

Thaw the puff pastry sheets in the refrigerator for 24–36 hours, or according to the directions on the package.

Trim the ends of the rhubarb stalks. Using a paring knife, pull away any strings of fibers visible at the tops and discard. Cut the stalks crosswise into 1/2-inch (12-mm) pieces. Put in a saucepan with 2/3 cup (5 oz/155 g) of the granulated sugar and let stand for 30 minutes.

Place the saucepan over medium heat and cook, stirring often, until the rhubarb is tender but not dissolving, 6–8 minutes. The rhubarb will release its juices. If it seems dry, add 2 or 3 teaspoons water. Set aside and let cool.

On a lightly floured work surface, roll out each puff pastry sheet into a 16-inch (40-cm) square, making sure there are no breaks or cracks in the pastry. Cut off the corners to make a rough circle. Place each circle on a baking sheet lined with parchment (baking) paper.

In a bowl, mix the rhubarb and strawberries together. Evenly divide the rhubarb-strawberry mixture in the center of each circle, leaving about 2 inches (5 cm) around the edge uncovered. Divide the remaining 1/3 cup (3 oz/95 g) granulated sugar between the fruit-topped circles, sprinkling it evenly on top. Fold up the uncovered edge, pleating it loosely and covering all but about a 5-inch (13-cm) circle of fruit in the center of the pastry. Place in the freezer and chill for 20 minutes. Meanwhile, preheat the oven to 350°F (180°C).

Remove the baking sheets from the freezer and immediately place in the oven. Bake until the crusts are puffed and golden brown, 20–25 minutes. Remove from the oven and let cool for 10 minutes on the pan on a wire rack. Carefully transfer to a cutting board. Using a fine-mesh sieve, sprinkle a light dusting of confectioners' sugar evenly over the top of each galette. Serve warm, cut into wedges.

2 sheets frozen puff pastry, each about 12 by 14 inches (30 by 35 cm) and 1/4 inch (6 mm) thick

10–12 rhubarb stalks, 1 1/2–2 lb (750 g–1 kg) total weight

1 cup (8 oz/250 g) granulated sugar

8 cups (2 lb/1 kg) strawberries, hulled and quartered if large or halved if small

Confectioners' (icing) sugar for dusting

SERVES 10–12

CHOCOLATE ESPRESSO CRÈMES WITH CANDIED CITRUS

For this remarkably easy and decadent treat, use semisweet chocolate containing at least 70 percent cacao. You can flavor the whipped cream with a touch of vanilla extract or even a pinch of finely grated fresh orange zest. Use small demitasse spoons for serving.

In a large saucepan over medium-high heat, bring 1½ cups (12 fl oz/375 ml) of the cream almost to a boil, until bubbles start to form on the surface. Remove from the heat and stir in the chocolate and espresso powder. Using a whisk, beat vigorously until the chocolate is melted and the mixture is silky smooth, about 1 minute. Divide the mixture evenly among 6 demitasse cups or ⅓-cup (3–fl oz/80-ml) ramekins. Cover loosely with plastic wrap and refrigerate until well chilled and the edges are firm, at least 6 hours or up to 24 hours. Remove from the refrigerator 15 minutes before serving.

To serve, in a bowl, using an electric mixer or a whisk, whip the remaining ½ cup (4 fl oz/125 ml) cream until soft peaks form. Garnish each dessert with a dollop of whipped cream and a few strips of orange peel.

Something on the side

Although these chocolatey treats are quite rich on their own, you can also serve them with rolled wafer cookies or biscotti on the side. Garnish with fresh chocolate shavings or a dusting of espresso powder in place of the candied orange peel, if you wish.

2 cups (16 fl oz/500 ml) heavy (double) cream

6 oz (185 g) semisweet (plain) chocolate, finely chopped

1 tablespoon instant espresso powder

Candied orange peel, cut into narrow strips, for garnish

SERVES 6

LEMON CUSTARDS WITH LEMON VERBENA CREAM

The crisp flavor of fresh lemon verbena leaves infuses the cream used to garnish this classic custard. Look for the herb at specialty stores or farmers' markets. If Meyer lemons are available for use in the custard, reduce the sugar by 2 tablespoons, since they are sweeter than regular lemons.

In the top of a double boiler set over, but not touching, barely simmering water, stir together the cornstarch, sugar, and salt. Add the boiling water and whisk until well blended, about 3 minutes. Remove the top of the double boiler and cook the cornstarch mixture directly over medium-low heat, stirring constantly, until thick and clear, about 5 minutes. Put the egg yolks in a bowl, whisk until blended, and then whisk in about ¼ cup (2 fl oz/60 ml) of the cornstarch mixture. Pour into the top of the double boiler and continue to cook directly over medium heat, stirring constantly, until thickened, 2–3 minutes. Remove from the heat and stir in the lemon zest and juice and the butter. Pour into individual ramekins or glasses and let cool for at least 2 hours at room temperature. (The custard can be prepared up to 1 day in advance and refrigerated. Bring to room temperature before serving.)

To make the lemon verbena cream, in a small saucepan over medium heat, bring the cream to a simmer. Stir in the sugar and lemon verbena leaves and cook, stirring, until the sugar dissolves, 2–3 minutes. Remove from the heat and let stand for 3–4 hours. Discard the leaves. Return the pan to the stove and bring the cream to a boil over medium-high heat, stirring constantly. Continue to cook until the cream has reduced by half and has thickened, about 5 minutes. Cool to warm or room temperature before serving.

Drizzle the cream over the custard and garnish each serving with a small sprig of lemon verbena. Serve at once.

⅓ cup (1½ oz/45 g) cornstarch (cornflour)

1¼ cups (10 oz/315 g) sugar

¼ teaspoon salt

1½ cups (12 fl oz/375 ml) boiling water

3 large egg yolks

½ teaspoon finely grated lemon zest

⅓ cup (3 fl oz/80 ml) fresh lemon juice (about 2 lemons)

2 tablespoons unsalted butter

Lemon Verbena Cream

1 cup (8 fl oz/250 ml) heavy (double) cream

¼ cup (2 oz/60 g) sugar

6–8 fresh lemon verbena leaves

6–8 fresh small lemon verbena sprigs for garnish

SERVES 6–8

FRUIT COMPOTE WITH BROWN SUGAR COOKIES Make this

sweet-tart compote of spring fruits and these crisp pan cookies a day before you plan to serve them, keeping your last-minute to-do list at a minimum. When ready to serve, break the cookie into free-form pieces and let guests spoon over the compote before taking a bite.

To make the compote, in a nonreactive saucepan over medium-high heat, combine the rhubarb, strawberries, butter, brown sugar, granulated sugar, vanilla bean, and lemon zest and juice. Bring to a boil, stirring gently, and then reduce the heat to low. Simmer until the fruits are soft, 10–12 minutes. Let cool and then discard the vanilla bean. Transfer the cooled compote to an airtight container and refrigerate. (The compote can be prepared up to 1 day in advance.)

To make the cookies, in a bowl, sift together the flour, baking soda, cloves, ginger, and salt. Set aside. In a stand mixer fitted with the paddle attachment, cream the butter and brown sugar on medium-high speed until smooth, about 3 minutes. Slowly stream in the maple syrup and continue to beat until well incorporated, about 2 minutes longer. Reduce the speed to low and add the flour mixture 1/2 cup (21/2 oz/75 g) at a time. Continue beating until the mixture comes together into a dough, about 3 minutes. Transfer the dough to a lightly floured work surface, divide it in half, and form each half into a disk 6 inches (15 cm) in diameter. Wrap each disk in plastic wrap and refrigerate for 1 hour.

Position a rack in the middle of the oven and a second rack in the upper third and preheat to 350°F (180°C). Line two 12-by-17-inch (30-by-43-cm) baking sheets with parchment (baking) paper. On a lightly floured work surface, roll out 1 dough disk into an oval about 1/2 inch (12 mm) thick. Transfer the dough to a prepared baking sheet and continue to roll until it is 1/8 inch (3 mm) thick. Sprinkle 1 tablespoon of the coarse sugar evenly over the surface. Repeat with the second dough disk.

Bake until firm and brittle, about 20 minutes, alternating the pans between the 2 oven racks halfway through baking. Let cool on a wire rack. (Once cool, the cookies can be wrapped and stored at room temperature for up to 1 day.)

To serve, spoon the compote into individual bowls. Break 1 pan cookie into 12 pieces and garnish each bowl with 2 pieces. Pass the second pan cookie, allowing guests to break off pieces.

Compote

6 stalks rhubarb, about
11/3 lb (655 g) total weight,
cut crosswise into 1/2-inch
(12-mm) pieces

2 cups (8 oz/250 g)
strawberries, hulled
and quartered

3 tablespoons unsalted butter

1/2 cup (31/2 oz/105 g) firmly
packed light brown sugar

1/2 cup (4 oz/125 g)
granulated sugar

1 vanilla bean, split lengthwise

Finely grated zest and
juice of 1 lemon

Brown Sugar Cookies

21/2 cups (121/2 oz/390 g)
all-purpose (plain) flour

2 teaspoons baking soda
(bicarbonate of soda)

1 teaspoon each ground
cloves and ground ginger

3/4 teaspoon salt

1 cup (8 oz/250 g) unsalted
butter, at room temperature

11/4 cups (9 oz/280 g) firmly
packed light brown sugar

1/3 cup (31/2 fl oz/105 ml)
maple syrup

2 tablespoons coarse sugar

SERVES 6

LEMON POUND CAKE

This classic lemon cake is best prepared a day in advance, which will allow the sugary lemon syrup time to infuse the cake with added moisture and flavor. Serve the cake with fresh sliced strawberries—a favorite springtime berry and a wonderful partner for lemons—and lightly whipped cream to spoon alongside.

Preheat the oven to 350°F (180°C). Lightly butter a 10-cup (2½-qt/2.5-l) Bundt pan. Dust with flour and tap out the excess. In a large bowl, sift together the flour, baking powder, and salt. Set aside.

In a stand mixer fitted with the paddle attachment, cream together the butter and cream cheese on medium-high speed until smooth, about 3 minutes. Reduce the speed to medium and add the sugar. Continue to beat until light and fluffy, about 2 minutes longer. Beat in the eggs one at a time, beating well after each addition. Remove the bowl from the mixer and, using a rubber spatula, fold in the flour mixture until incorporated. Stir in the vanilla, lemon zest, and lemon juice.

Pour the batter into the prepared pan and smooth the top with the spatula. Bake until a toothpick inserted in the center comes out clean, about 1 hour. Transfer to a wire rack and let cool in the pan for 30 minutes.

While the cake is baking, make the lemon syrup: In a nonreactive saucepan over medium heat, combine the lemon zest, lemon juice, and sugar, stirring until the sugar is dissolved. Bring to a boil and then reduce the heat to low. Simmer until reduced by one-third, 10–15 minutes. Remove from the heat and let stand at room temperature until ready to use.

To loosen the cake, tap the sides of the pan gently on the counter. Invert a flat cake plate or pedestal over the pan and invert the plate and the pan together. Tap the bottom of the pan with your hand and then lift off the pan. While the cake is still warm, poke holes in the surface with a toothpick and brush the cake all over with the lemon syrup, allowing the cake to absorb the syrup before applying more. Let the cake cool for 30 minutes longer before serving. (The cake can be baked and glazed up to 12 hours in advance. Let cool to room temperature and tent loosely with plastic wrap.)

Just before serving, slice the cake into wedges and garnish with lemon slices.

3 cups (12 oz/375 g) cake (soft-wheat) flour

2 teaspoons baking powder

1 teaspoon salt

1½ cups (12 oz/375 g) unsalted butter, at room temperature

½ lb (250 g) cream cheese, at room temperature

2 cups (1 lb/500 g) sugar

6 large eggs

2 teaspoons vanilla extract

1 tablespoon finely grated lemon zest

¼ cup (2 fl oz/60 ml) fresh lemon juice

Lemon Syrup

1 tablespoon finely grated lemon zest

½ cup (4 fl oz/125 ml) fresh lemon juice

½ cup (4 oz/125 g) sugar

Lemon slices for garnish

SERVES 6

FROZEN TIRAMISU

Here, the popular coffee-and-cocoa-laced Italian dessert is made with ice cream in place of mascarpone cheese, and assembled in individual molds to simplify serving. Prepare the desserts the night before your dinner, so that all you have to do is slip them free, garnish, and serve.

Microwave the ice cream until just softened, 30–45 seconds on medium power. Alternatively, set the ice cream on the counter until soft, about 20 minutes. Select four ¾-cup (6–fl oz/180-ml) custard molds or ramekins. Line each mold with a sheet of plastic wrap, allowing a 2-inch (5-cm) overhang.

In a small bowl, combine the coffee and coffee liqueur.

Place ¼ cup (¼ oz/7 g) of the ladyfinger crumbs in the bottom of each prepared mold. Moisten the crumbs with 2 teaspoons of the coffee mixture. Top with 2 tablespoons of the ice cream and spread the surface smooth. Using a fine-mesh sieve, lightly dust the ice cream with cocoa powder. Repeat the layers. Add a final layer of ladyfinger crumbs, gently pressing them into the ice cream to form a flat surface. Drizzle the remaining coffee mixture over the surface, dividing evenly. Fold the overhanging plastic wrap over the top, covering completely. Place the molds in the freezer for at least 2 hours or up to 24 hours.

When ready to serve, remove the molds from the freezer and let sit for 15 minutes at room temperature. Unwrap the plastic and invert each mold onto an individual dessert plate. Pull on the edges of the plastic wrap to help unmold each tiramisu, then peel off the plastic wrap. Dust the tops with cocoa powder and sprinkle with some chocolate shavings. Serve at once.

1 cup (8 fl oz/250 ml) vanilla ice cream

½ cup (4 fl oz/125 ml) strong coffee

2 tablespoons coffee liqueur

1 package (3 oz/90 g) ladyfingers, broken up into large crumbs, about 3 cups

Cocoa powder for dusting

Semisweet (plain) chocolate shavings for garnish

SERVES 4

summer

drinks and starters

soups and salads

mains and sides

desserts

CITRUS CAIPIRINHAS

Select 4 old-fashioned or short glasses. Put 1 lemon quarter and 1 tablespoon of the sugar in each glass. Muddle well with a muddler or the handle of a wooden spoon. Add ¼ cup (2 fl oz/60 ml) of the cachaça to each glass, stir well, and then fill the glasses with ice. Garnish each glass with a lemon slice and serve at once.

1 lemon, quartered

4 tablespoons superfine (caster) sugar

1 cup (8 fl oz/250 ml) cachaça

Ice cubes

4 lemon slices for garnish

SERVES 4

CUCUMBER-LIME COOLERS

Select 4 old-fashioned or short glasses. Combine ¼ cup (2 fl oz/60 ml) of the lime juice and 1½ tablespoons of sugar in each glass and stir to dissolve the sugar. Fill the glasses with ice and then top each glass with ¾ cup (6 fl oz/180 ml) of the sparkling water. Garnish each glass with several cucumber and lime slices and serve at once.

1 cup (8 fl oz/250 ml) fresh lime juice (4–5 large limes)

6 tablespoons superfine (caster) sugar

Ice cubes

1 bottle (24 fl oz/750 ml) sparkling water, chilled

Thin cucumber and lime slices for garnish

SERVES 4

MANGO-GUAVA SPARKLERS
In hot summer weather, a combination of fruit nectars with a splash of lime juice and sparkling water makes a refreshing aperitif to welcome your guests. A mango cube or two threaded onto a toothpick can replace the strawberry garnish.

Select 8 tall glasses. Put a few ice cubes in each glass. Pour ¼ cup (2 fl oz/60 ml) of the mango nectar, ½ cup (4 fl oz/125 ml) of the guava nectar, 1 tablespoon lime juice, and about ½ cup (4 fl oz/125 ml) of the sparkling water into each glass and stir. To garnish, balance a strawberry on the rim of each glass. Serve at once.

Refreshing fruit sparklers

Any type of fruit juice or nectar mixed with sparkling water makes a welcome nonalcoholic offering at a party. You can mix each drink separately, or make a big batch and pour it into a pitcher or punch bowl with ice and fresh fruit.

Ice cubes

2 cups (16 fl oz/500 ml) mango nectar

4 cups (32 fl oz/1 l) guava nectar

½ cup (4 fl oz/125 ml) fresh lime juice (3–4 limes)

4 cups (32 fl oz/1 l) sparkling water

8 strawberries, slit lengthwise nearly in half with stem end intact, for garnish

SERVES 8

WATERMELON AND TEQUILA FRESCAS
Here, fresh fruit puréed with a little ice and spiked with tequila is a colorful alternative to the usual margarita. The watermelon can be prepared a day in advance and kept covered in the refrigerator until ready to use.

Select 8 tumblers or old-fashioned glasses. Set aside 8 watermelon cubes for garnish. In a blender, combine half each of the remaining watermelon, the ice, the lime juice, and the tequila. Purée until smooth. Pour into 4 of the glasses. Repeat to make 4 more drinks. To garnish, sandwich a reserved watermelon cube between 2 mint leaves on a cocktail pick and balance it on the rim of each glass. Serve at once.

Chilling glasses

To ensure that drinks stay cold, place the glasses in the freezer or refrigerator for several hours before using. Or, for a quick chill, fill the glasses with ice and water, let them sit for a few minutes, and then dump them out just before pouring in the drink.

1 small seedless watermelon, about 2½ lb (1.25 kg), flesh removed from rind and cut into 1-inch (2.5-cm) cubes

2 cups (16 oz/500 g) crushed ice

½ cup (4 fl oz/125 ml) fresh lime juice (3–4 limes)

1½ cups (12 fl oz/375 ml) tequila

16 fresh mint leaves for garnish

SERVES 8

CLASSIC SANGRIA

In a punch bowl or pitcher, combine the wine, ginger ale, and orange juice and stir to mix. Add the citrus slices and stir again. Cover and refrigerate for at least 2 hours or up to 12 hours to blend the flavors.

When ready to serve, add ice to the punch bowl and let guests serve themselves.

1 bottle (24 fl oz/750 ml) dry red wine

1 bottle (24 fl oz/750 ml) dry ginger ale

3 cups (24 fl oz/750 ml) fresh orange juice

1 orange, thinly sliced crosswise

1 lemon, thinly sliced crosswise

Ice cubes

SERVES 6–8

PLUM AND NECTARINE SANGRIA

In a large pitcher, combine the plum and nectarine wedges, nectarine nectar, orange liqueur, and white wine. Stir well, cover, and refrigerate for at least 2 hours or up to 12 hours to blend the flavors.

To serve, fill glasses with ice cubes and add the wine mixture, dividing evenly. Top off each glass with sparkling water. Serve at once.

3 plums, halved, pitted, and cut into thin wedges

3 nectarines, halved, pitted, and cut into thin wedges

1 can (12 fl oz/375 ml) nectarine or peach nectar

¼ cup (2 fl oz/60 ml) orange liqueur

1 bottle (24 fl oz/750 ml) dry white wine

Ice cubes

1 bottle (24 fl oz/750 ml) sparkling water, chilled

SERVES 6

PEACH BELLINI

Select 4 Champagne flutes. In a blender, purée the peaches until completely smooth. Taste and add the sugar if needed. Fill each flute about one-third full of the purée. Top with the sparkling wine. Serve at once.

2 ripe peaches, preferably white, peeled, halved, and pitted

About 1 tablespoon superfine (caster) sugar, if needed

1 bottle (24 fl oz/750 ml) Champagne, Prosecco, or sparkling wine, chilled

SERVES 4

CHERRY SPARKLERS

Select 4 highball glasses. Put several ice cubes in each glass. Pour ¾ cup (6 fl oz/180 ml) of the cherry juice over the ice in each glass, and then top with about ¼ cup (2 fl oz/60 ml) of the sparkling water. Garnish each glass with a cherry and serve at once.

Ice cubes

3 cups (24 fl oz/750 ml) cherry juice, preferably fresh

1 cup (8 fl oz/250 ml) sparkling water

4 fresh cherries with stems intact for garnish

SERVES 4

HONEYDEW AND MINT AGUA FRESCA

This easy Latin-inspired drink, made of puréed fruit and fresh mint mixed with sparkling water, is perfect for a summer day. You can use watermelon or cantaloupe in place of the honeydew, or substitute limes for the lemons.

Cut the honeydew melons in half and remove and discard the seeds. Using a metal spoon, scoop out the flesh into a large bowl. Working in batches, purée the honeydew melon in a blender or food processor. As each batch is finished, transfer it to another large bowl. Add the lemon juice, sugar, and mint leaves to the purée and stir to combine until the sugar is fully dissolved. Cover the bowl and let stand at room temperature for at least 1 hour or up to 4 hours to blend the flavors.

When ready to serve, pour the melon mixture through a medium-mesh sieve into a large pitcher or jar. Add the sparkling water, lemon slices, and ice and stir well. Pour or ladle into glasses and garnish each glass with a sprig of fresh mint.

2 honeydew melons, about 12 lb (6 kg) total weight

Juice of 4 lemons

¾ cup (6 oz/185 g) sugar

1 cup (1 oz/30 g) crushed fresh mint leaves

3 cups (24 fl oz/750 ml) sparkling water, chilled

3 lemons, thinly sliced

Ice cubes

10–12 fresh mint sprigs for garnish

SERVES 10–12

CLASSIC MARGARITAS

Blended or on the rocks, with or without salt—margaritas can vary. But always start with good tequila, fresh lime juice, and a quality orange liqueur. For a fruity variation, mix in some fresh strawberries, hulled and trimmed, before puréeing each batch.

Select 8 margarita glasses or tumblers. Spread a layer of salt on a small, flat plate. Working with 1 glass at a time, run a lime wedge around the rim of the glass to moisten it and then dip the rim into the salt to coat it evenly. Repeat with the remaining glasses, using the same lime wedge to moisten all the rims.

Mix the drinks in 2 batches: Fill a blender half full with ice. Add ¾ cup (6 fl oz/185 ml) of the tequila, ½ cup (4 fl oz/125 ml) of the lime juice, ¼ cup (2 fl oz/60 ml) of the orange liqueur, and ½ cup (4 fl oz/125 ml) of the frozen limeade concentrate. Purée until well blended. Divide the mixture evenly among 4 of the glasses. Garnish each glass with a lime wedge. Serve at once. Repeat to make the second batch.

Kosher salt for coating the glass rims

9 lime wedges

Ice cubes

1½ cups (12 fl oz/375 ml) 100 percent agave tequila

1 cup (8 fl oz/250 ml) fresh lime juice

½ cup (4 fl oz/125 ml) orange liqueur

1 cup (8 fl oz/250 ml) frozen limeade concentrate

SERVES 8

PARMESAN-ZUCCHINI FRITTATA

Frittatas are quick and easy to assemble and cook and can be served at room temperature, making them ideal cocktail party fare. They're also well suited for a brunch gathering and pair nicely with ham or bacon. This recipe calls for zucchini, but you can use any of your favorite summer squash varieties in its place.

Using the large holes of a box grater-shredder, grate the zucchini. Lay the grated zucchini on paper towels to drain briefly.

In a large bowl, whisk together the eggs, half-and-half, cheese, salt, and pepper just until blended. Stir in the drained zucchini.

Preheat the broiler (grill). In a flameproof 10-inch (25-cm) frying pan over medium-high heat, melt the butter with the olive oil. When the butter foams, add the onion and sauté until translucent, 2–3 minutes. Add the garlic, thyme, and parsley and sauté for 1 minute.

Pour in the egg mixture, reduce the heat to low, and cook until the eggs are just firm around the edges, 3–4 minutes. Using a spatula, lift the edges and tilt the pan to let the uncooked portion flow underneath. Continue cooking until the eggs are nearly set, 4–5 minutes more.

Slip the pan under the broiler about 4 inches (10 cm) from the heat source and broil (grill) until the top sets and browns lightly, about 2 minutes. Remove from the broiler and slide onto a cutting board; let cool. Cut into 1-inch (2.5-cm) pieces. Garnish with parsley and serve at room temperature.

2 zucchini (courgettes)

6 large eggs

2 tablespoons half-and-half (half cream)

¼ cup (1 oz/30 g) grated Parmesan cheese

¾ teaspoon salt

½ teaspoon freshly ground pepper

2 tablespoons unsalted butter

1 tablespoon extra-virgin olive oil

2 tablespoons finely chopped yellow onion

1 clove garlic, minced

1 teaspoon chopped fresh thyme

¼ cup (⅓ oz/10 g) chopped fresh flat-leaf (Italian) parsley, plus extra for garnish

SERVES 10–12

CORN FRITTERS WITH ROMESCO SAUCE

These bite-sized fritters are best served hot out of the frying pan, but they are nearly as delicious at room temperature. Their subtle sweetness is the perfect foil for the nutty yet piquant flavor of romesco sauce. The sauce can be made well in advance; store it in an airtight container in the refrigerator for up to 1 week.

To make the romesco sauce, preheat the oven to 325°F (165°C). Cut off the upper one-third of the garlic head and discard. Core the tomatoes. Put the garlic, tomatoes, and bell pepper in a baking dish just large enough to hold them and drizzle with the olive oil. Roast, uncovered, until the pepper and tomatoes collapse and the garlic cloves are tender, 30–45 minutes. Remove from the oven and let cool.

Peel the tomatoes. Squeeze the garlic pulp from its papery sheaths. Halve and seed the bell pepper. In a food processor, combine the tomatoes, garlic pulp, bell pepper, almonds, paprika, vinegar, bread, the 1 teaspoon salt, and the ¼ teaspoon cayenne and process until puréed. Taste and add more salt and cayenne, if desired. Transfer to a bowl, cover, and refrigerate until serving.

To make the fritters, one at a time, hold an ear of corn upright, stem end down, in a shallow dish. Using a sharp knife, slice straight down between the kernels and the cob to remove the kernels, rotating the ear a quarter turn after each cut.

In a large bowl, combine the green onions, flour, baking powder, salt, and pepper and stir to mix well. Add the egg, milk, and corn kernels and stir just to combine.

In a large frying pan over medium-high heat, warm 2 tablespoons of the oil. When the oil is hot, drop in a heaping tablespoonful of the fritter batter, then press down to flatten.

Repeat to form more fritters, being careful not to crowd the pan. Cook until golden on the first side, about 3 minutes. Turn over and cook until the second side is golden, about 2 minutes longer. Using a slotted spoon, transfer to paper towels to drain. Repeat with the remaining batter, adding more oil to the pan as needed for each batch.

Place the bowl of romesco sauce in the center of a platter and surround with the fritters. Serve warm or at room temperature.

Romesco Sauce

1 head garlic

3 large tomatoes

1 red bell pepper (capsicum)

1 tablespoon extra-virgin olive oil

⅓ cup (2 oz/60 g) blanched almonds, toasted

1 teaspoon sweet paprika

2 tablespoons sherry vinegar

3 slices day-old baguette, cut into ½-inch (12-mm) cubes

1 teaspoon salt

¼ teaspoon cayenne pepper

Fritters

3 ears of corn, shucked

10 green (spring) onions, including pale green tops, minced

1 cup (5 oz/155 g) all-purpose (plain) flour

1½ teaspoons baking powder

1 teaspoon each salt and freshly ground pepper

1 large egg, lightly beaten

⅔ cup (5 fl oz/160 ml) whole milk

About 6 tablespoons (3 fl oz/90 ml) canola, grape seed, or sunflower oil

SERVES 12–14

SHRIMP, CANTALOUPE, AND FRESH HERB SKEWERS

Cubes of sweet cantaloupe are paired with marinated shrimp for a passed hors d'oeuvre that is flavorful, refreshing, and easy to prepare. Look for medium-sized shrimp, which are just the right size for a satisfying bite. This seafood dish pairs well with a citrusy cocktail, such as a margarita (page 89).

In a bowl large enough to accommodate the shrimp, stir together the coconut cream, fish sauce, lime juice, sesame oil, chives, chopped mint, and chile. Set aside.

Bring a large pot of salted water to a boil over high heat. Add the shrimp and cook until they turn pink and begin to curl, about 2 minutes. Using a slotted spoon, transfer the shrimp to the bowl holding the coconut cream mixture and toss to coat evenly. Let cool to room temperature, cover with plastic wrap, and refrigerate for at least 2 hours or up to 8 hours.

Cut the cantaloupe half into 6 wedges. Working with 1 wedge at a time, remove the rind and cut the wedge into 6 equal pieces. You should have a total of 36 cubes of cantaloupe, each about ¾ inch (2 cm) wide.

Soak 36 wooden skewers in water to cover in a shallow baking dish for 30 minutes and then drain. Remove the shrimp from the refrigerator and drain in a colander. To assemble the skewers, thread 1 shrimp and 1 piece of cantaloupe onto each skewer. Place the skewers in a single layer on a rimmed baking sheet, cover with plastic wrap, and refrigerate until ready to serve. (The shrimp can be skewered up to 4 hours in advance.)

To serve, arrange the skewers down the center of a narrow platter or tray, positioning them so that the skewer ends are easy to grasp. Garnish the platter with mint sprigs.

2 tablespoons coconut cream, scooped from the top of an unshaken can of coconut milk

1 tablespoon Thai fish sauce

2 teaspoons fresh lime juice

1 teaspoon Asian sesame oil

2 tablespoons snipped fresh chives

2 tablespoons chopped fresh mint, plus sprigs for garnish

1 small red chile, seeded and minced

1 lb (500 g) medium shrimp (prawns), peeled and deveined (36 shrimp)

½ small cantaloupe

SERVES 10–12

GRILLED CALAMARI SKEWERS

Calamari, or squid, can be found in the fresh or frozen fish section of many markets, making it easy to prepare these simple appetizers. If you can't find full bodies, use calamari rings, threading several onto each skewer.

In a shallow baking dish, whisk together the soy sauce, wine, garlic, ginger, and brown sugar until the sugar dissolves. Rinse the calamari bodies and pat dry with paper towels. Cut the bodies in half lengthwise, add to the dish, and turn to coat well. Cover and refrigerate for at least 1 hour or up to 4 hours. Soak 36 wooden skewers in water for at least 30 minutes.

Prepare a charcoal or gas grill for direct grilling over high heat. Lightly oil the grill rack and a grill basket. Drain the skewers and carefully thread the calamari onto them, discarding the marinade. Arrange as many skewers as will fit side by side in the grill basket and place on the grill rack. Grill, turning once, until the calamari are opaque throughout, about 2 minutes on each side. Transfer to a platter and repeat with the remaining skewers. Serve hot or warm.

3 tablespoons soy sauce

1 tablespoon dry red wine

2 cloves garlic, crushed

2 teaspoons peeled and grated fresh ginger

1 teaspoon firmly packed light brown sugar

1½ lb (750 g) cleaned calamari bodies

SERVES 10–12

SCALLOP CEVICHE

Sea scallops, which are bigger than the bay variety, are ideal for this dish. Use the freshest scallops you can find, and be sure to trim off any hard tissue on the side of the scallops before using. Garnish the dish with fresh cilantro and lime slices.

Rinse and dry the scallops and cut horizontally into slices ¼ inch (6 mm) thick. Thread the scallop pieces onto small wooden skewers, using about 5 scallop slices per skewer. Arrange the skewers in a single layer in a shallow nonreactive dish. Cut the jalapeño in half, remove the seeds, and mince (you should have about 2 tablespoons). Sprinkle the scallops with 1 tablespoon of the minced chile, the cilantro, salt, ginger, and lime zest. Carefully pour the lime juice over the scallops and turn the skewers several times.

Cover with plastic wrap and refrigerate for at least 3 hours or up to 12 hours before serving, turning occasionally.

About 30 minutes before serving, turn the skewers several times, then sprinkle with the remaining chile, the onion, and the tomato.

Arrange the scallop skewers on a platter and serve.

1¼ lb (625 g) sea scallops

1 jalapeño chile

¼ cup (⅓ oz/10 g) minced fresh cilantro (fresh coriander)

½ teaspoon salt

2 teaspoons peeled and grated fresh ginger

Grated zest of 1 lime

½ cup (4 fl oz/125 ml) fresh lime juice

½ small red onion, minced

1 small tomato, peeled, seeded, and minced

SERVES 14–16

TENDERLOIN AND HEIRLOOM TOMATO CANAPÉS

Few cuts of beef are as succulent as beef tenderloin, which, when thinly sliced, makes an elegant canapé topping. Here, in the spirit of summer, the slices are topped with chopped heirloom tomatoes and fresh basil. Although you can serve these bite-sized hors d'oeuvres warm, they are best at room temperature.

Preheat the oven to 350°F (180°C). Arrange the bread slices in a single layer on a rimmed baking sheet. Bake, turning once halfway through baking, until lightly golden, about 20 minutes. Remove from the oven and set aside. Raise the oven temperature to 450°F (230°C).

In a small bowl, whisk together 2 tablespoons of the olive oil, 1½ teaspoons of the salt, and 1 teaspoon of the pepper. Brush the oil mixture on all sides of the tenderloin and place the tenderloin on a rack in a shallow roasting pan just large enough to accommodate it.

Roast the tenderloin until an instant-read thermometer inserted into the thickest part of the fillet registers 120°F (49°C) for rare, about 20 minutes; 130°F (54°C) for medium-rare, about 25 minutes; or 140°F (60°C) for medium,

about 30 minutes. Transfer the beef to a cutting board, cover loosely with aluminum foil, and let rest for 15–20 minutes. Carve against the grain into thin slices.

Chop the tomatoes and place them in a colander to drain for 10 minutes. Sort through the basil leaves and set aside 30 small whole leaves. Cut the remaining basil leaves into thin strips.

In a large bowl, combine the remaining 2 tablespoons olive oil, 1 teaspoon salt, and ½ teaspoon pepper. Add the tomatoes and sliced basil and turn gently to coat the tomatoes evenly.

To assemble, place a slice or two of beef on a toasted baguette slice and top with a teaspoon of tomatoes and a basil leaf. Arrange the canapés on a platter and serve.

30 baguettes slices,
¼ inch (6 mm) thick
(about 1 large baguette)

4 tablespoons (2 fl oz/60 ml)
extra-virgin olive oil

2½ teaspoons salt

1½ teaspoons freshly
ground pepper

1½–2 lb (750 g–1 kg) piece
beef tenderloin, trimmed
of fat and sinew

1½ lb (750 g) mixed
heirloom tomatoes

2 cups (2 oz/60 g) fresh
basil leaves

SERVES 12–14

SHRIMP AND CRAB COCKTAIL

Individually packed jars make serving shellfish outside easy. The cocktails can be prepared up to twelve hours ahead and stored in the refrigerator. Use ice packs for transport and keep the cocktails cold until ready to serve. Look for ready-to-serve shrimp and crabmeat at seafood counters.

To make the vinaigrette, in a small bowl, whisk together the olive oil, lemon zest, lemon juice, mustard, garlic, oregano, and saffron. Season to taste with salt and pepper.

Wash and thoroughly dry six 1-pint (16–fl oz/500-ml) canning jars with glass lids and wire bale closures. Place half of the shrimp in the bottoms of the 6 jars, dividing them evenly. Top with half of the celery, green onions, crabmeat, and fennel slices. Repeat the layers, starting with the shrimp and finishing with the fennel slices. Drizzle the vinaigrette into the jars, dividing it evenly. Garnish the top of each jar with a lemon slice and a bay leaf. Close the lids and refrigerate the jars for 2 hours or up to 12 hours to blend the flavors.

Just before serving, rock each jar back and forth a few times to distribute the vinaigrette. Serve cold directly from the jars.

Layered summer salads

To make your favorite salads travel friendly, use mason jars or other wide-mouthed jars for both storage and presentation. Layer any heavier items on the bottom of the jar and top with additional ingredients in order of weight. Add the vinaigrette last. Shake the jars just before serving to mix.

Vinaigrette

¾ cup (6 fl oz/180 ml) olive oil

Grated zest of 1 lemon

¼ cup (2 fl oz/60 ml) fresh lemon juice

1 teaspoon Dijon mustard

1 clove garlic, finely chopped

2 teaspoons chopped fresh oregano

Pinch of saffron threads

Kosher salt and freshly ground pepper

1 lb (500 g) peeled cooked shrimp (prawns)

3 celery stalks, thinly sliced

3 green (spring) onions, including tender green tops, chopped

1 lb (500 g) crabmeat, picked over for shell fragments

1 fennel bulb, trimmed, quartered lengthwise, cored, and sliced crosswise paper-thin

6 thin lemon slices

6 small bay leaves

SERVES 6

CUCUMBER-DILL SOUP

A chilled soup is a great beginning for a picnic at the beach. For foolproof transport, select a container with a tight-fitting lid that permits easy serving. Fill with the soup, cap tightly, place upright in an ice chest, and secure in place with bags of ice or cool packs. To serve, pour the soup into widemouthed glasses or cups so that guests can sip it.

Coarsely chop 5 of the cucumber halves and transfer to a large bowl. Add the yogurt, lemon juice, green onions, dill, garlic, caraway seeds, salt, and white pepper. Stir to combine, cover with plastic wrap, and set aside at room temperature for 1 hour to blend the flavors. Dice the remaining cucumber half and set aside until ready to serve.

In a blender, purée the cucumber mixture until smooth. With the machine running, slowly add the stock and purée until it is fully incorporated, about 30 seconds. Transfer to a pitcher, cover with plastic wrap, and refrigerate until chilled, about 2 hours. (The soup can be prepared up to 12 hours in advance and stored in an airtight container in the refrigerator. If it separates, simply stir it until emulsified.)

Just before serving, stir in the diced cucumber and olive oil. Pour the soup into widemouthed glasses or cups and serve at once.

A beach-friendly menu

For a summer lunch or light dinner at the beach, pair this cooling soup with the Shrimp and Crab Cocktail (page 103) and the Pepper, Tomato, Olive, and Manchego Chopped Salad (page 112). For wine, bring a chilled Sauvignon Blanc or Rosé.

3 English (hothouse) cucumbers, peeled, halved lengthwise, and seeded

1 cup (8 oz/250 g) Greek-style or other thick, whole-milk plain yogurt

1 tablespoon fresh lemon juice

3 green (spring) onions, including tender green tops, chopped

3 tablespoons chopped fresh dill

1 clove garlic, chopped

1 teaspoon caraway seeds, crushed

1 teaspoon kosher salt

1/4 teaspoon ground white pepper

1 cup (8 fl oz/250 ml) vegetable stock or reduced-sodium vegetable broth

2 tablespoons fruity extra-virgin olive oil

SERVES 6

CAPRESE SALAD

Place the tomatoes on a cutting board, stem side down. Using a sharp knife, make 4 evenly spaced slits crosswise in each tomato, stopping about ½ inch (12 mm) from the bottom.

Cut the mozzarella into 32 thin, uniform slices. Working with 1 tomato at a time, insert 1 mozzarella slice and 1 basil leaf into each slit.

When ready to serve, place the prepared tomatoes on a platter. Drizzle with the olive oil and vinegar and season with the salt and pepper. Serve at once.

8 tomatoes

4 balls fresh mozzarella cheese, about ¾ lb (375 g) total weight

32 fresh basil leaves

Extra-virgin olive oil for drizzling

Aged balsamic vinegar for drizzling

Sea salt and freshly ground pepper

SERVES 8

ORZO SALAD WITH BASIL AND HEIRLOOM TOMATOES

Cut large or medium tomatoes into ½-inch (12-mm) cubes. Cut the cherry tomatoes in half. Set aside.

Bring a large pot of salted water to a boil. Add the orzo. When the water returns to a boil, reduce the heat to medium and cook until the pasta is al dente, about 9 minutes or according to package directions. Drain and place in a large bowl. (The orzo can be prepared up to 6 hours in advance, tossed with a small amount of olive oil to keep it from sticking, and refrigerated. Bring to room temperature before serving.)

Add the tomatoes, 1½ teaspoons salt, the olive oil, vinegar, and pepper and turn gently until well mixed. Add the snipped basil and turn again. Garnish with the basil leaves and serve at room temperature.

1 lb (500 g) mixed heirloom tomatoes of various sizes, including cherry tomatoes

Salt

3 cups (21 oz/655 g) orzo pasta

2 tablespoons extra-virgin olive oil

1 teaspoon red wine vinegar

1 teaspoon freshly ground pepper

½ cup (½ oz/15 g) fresh basil leaves, snipped into small pieces, plus 4–6 whole leaves for garnish

SERVES 6–8

FIELD GREENS WITH HOMEMADE CROUTONS

These croutons, made by browning cubes cut from a day-old baguette in garlic-flavored oil and seasoning them with sea salt and thyme, can be made a day in advance and added to the salad just before serving. Make an extra batch; they always prove popular. You can also use them as a garnish for soups.

Cut the bread slices into 1-inch (2.5-cm) cubes. In a frying pan over medium heat, warm 1/3 cup (3 fl oz/80 ml) of the olive oil. Add the garlic, reduce the heat to low, and sauté until golden, 2–3 minutes, being careful not to let it burn. Using a slotted spoon, remove the garlic and discard.

Add the bread cubes to the garlic oil and return the pan to low heat. Sauté slowly, turning once, until golden and crusty, 4–5 minutes on each side. Sprinkle with the fine sea salt and the thyme, toss briefly, and transfer the croutons to paper towels to drain. Let cool.

In a large serving bowl, combine the mustard and the remaining 2/3 cup (5 fl oz/170 ml) olive oil and mix together with a fork until thickened, about 2 minutes. Mix in the red wine vinegar, balsamic vinegar, coarse sea salt, and pepper.

Just before serving, add the field greens and toss well to coat generously with the vinaigrette. Add half of the croutons and toss again to coat. Garnish the salad with the remaining croutons.

12 slices day-old baguette, each 1 inch (2.5 cm) thick

1 cup (8 fl oz/250 ml) extra-virgin olive oil

2 cloves garlic, crushed

3/4 teaspoon fine sea salt

1 tablespoon minced fresh thyme

1 tablespoon Dijon mustard

1/3 cup (3 fl oz/80 ml) red wine vinegar

1 1/2 tablespoons balsamic vinegar

1 1/2 teaspoons coarse sea salt

1 1/2 teaspoons freshly ground pepper

2 lb (1 kg) mixed young field greens or a mixture of field greens and baby spinach

SERVES 12–14

CUCUMBER RIBBONS WITH TOMATOES, RICOTTA SALATA, AND OLIVES

Peel the cucumbers and cut in half lengthwise. Using a small spoon, scoop out the seeds (there will be very few) and discard them. Cut each half in half crosswise. Using a vegetable peeler or mandoline, cut the cucumbers lengthwise into ribbons about 1/8 inch (3 mm) thick. Halve the olives lengthwise. Core and halve the tomatoes, then scoop out the seeds. Dice the tomatoes.

In a large salad bowl, toss together the cucumber ribbons and tomatoes. Mound them on a serving platter. Scatter the olives, cheese, and thyme over the top. Drizzle with the olive oil and vinegar and season to taste with salt and pepper. Serve at once.

2 English (hothouse) cucumbers, about 2 lb (1 kg) total weight

1/2 cup (2 1/2 oz/75 g) pitted Kalamata olives

3 tomatoes

1/4 lb (125 g) ricotta salata, cut into shavings

2 tablespoons chopped fresh thyme

3 tablespoons olive oil

1 tablespoon red wine vinegar

Salt and freshly ground pepper

SERVES 8

SLICED TOMATOES WITH AVOCADO, ONION, AND PARSLEY

In a bowl, toss the avocado slices with the lemon juice. On a large platter, arrange the tomato slices, slightly overlapping, in a single layer. Scatter the onion and avocado slices over the top. Drizzle with the olive oil and any lemon juice that is left from the avocados. Sprinkle with salt, pepper, and the parsley. Serve at once.

3 avocados, halved, pitted, peeled, and thinly sliced

Juice of 1 lemon

8 assorted heirloom tomatoes, thinly sliced

1 small red onion, thinly sliced

1/4 cup (2 fl oz/60 ml) fruity extra-virgin olive oil

Kosher salt and freshly ground pepper

2 tablespoons coarsely chopped fresh flat-leaf (Italian) parsley

SERVES 10–12

PEPPER, TOMATO, OLIVE, AND MANCHEGO CHOPPED SALAD

To make the vinaigrette, in a large salad bowl, whisk together the olive oil, vinegar, mustard, garlic, salt, and pepper.

Add the bell peppers, tomatoes, celery, olives, onion, parsley, thyme, and cheese to the vinaigrette in the bowl. Toss until all the ingredients are coated with the vinaigrette. Transfer to an airtight container and refrigerate for up to 2 hours before serving. (The vegetables for the salad can be prepared up to 12 hours in advance and refrigerated. You can mix the vinaigrette at the same time and then combine it with the salad a couple of hours before serving.)

Chopped salads

Easy to make and delicious to eat, chopped salads are a crowd-friendly alternative to leafy greens. Choose firmer lettuces, such as romaine, radicchio, and endive, wash and dry, and chop into strips using a chef's knife. Add a protein (such as diced cheese, turkey, hard-boiled egg, or nuts), chopped vegetables, and fresh herbs, and then toss with your favorite vinaigrette.

Vinaigrette

¼ cup (2 fl oz/60 ml) olive oil

3 tablespoons sherry vinegar

1 teaspoon Dijon mustard

1 clove garlic, minced

¼ teaspoon kosher salt

½ teaspoon freshly ground pepper

1 small yellow bell pepper (capsicum), seeded and diced

1 small orange bell pepper (capsicum), seeded and diced

2 cups (12 oz/375 g) cherry tomatoes, stemmed and halved

4 celery stalks, thinly sliced

¾ cup (3 oz/90 g) pitted large Spanish green olives, quartered

¼ cup (1½ oz/45 g) finely chopped red onion

1 tablespoon chopped fresh flat-leaf (Italian) parsley

1 teaspoon chopped fresh thyme

½ lb (250 g) Manchego cheese, cut into ¼-inch (6-mm) cubes

SERVES 6

LOBSTER SALAD WITH CHAMPAGNE VINAIGRETTE

You can use either whole lobsters or lobster tails to make this elegant salad, fantastic for a summer lunch or dinner. Serve it on a bed of greens, such as field greens and baby arugula leaves, and fresh herbs, which makes for an attractive presentation and enhances the flavor. Pair with a crisp white wine.

If using frozen lobster tails, bring a large pot three-fourths full of water to a boil over high heat. Add the coarse sea salt. Put the lobster tails in the pot and boil them until the shells are bright red and the meat is almost opaque throughout, about 8 minutes.

Meanwhile, ready a large bowl full of ice. When the lobster tails are done, transfer them immediately to the tub and cover with ice. (This quick cooling causes the flesh to pull away from the shell, making it easier to remove the meat.) Leave in the ice for 30 minutes. Remove the meat from the tails.

Whether using fresh or frozen, cut the lobster meat into generous bite-sized pieces. Set aside.

In a large bowl, combine 2 tablespoons of the vinegar, the fresh lemon juice, 2 tablespoons of the olive oil, the fine sea salt, the pepper, and the minced tarragon and mix well. Add the lobster meat and gently turn the pieces in the vinaigrette until well coated.

Divide the mixed greens and herbs evenly among individual shallow bowls or salad plates. Place about ½ cup (3 oz/90 g) of the lobster salad atop each bed of greens. Add the remaining 1½ tablespoons olive oil and ½ tablespoon vinegar to the bowl, mix well, and drizzle a little over each serving. Serve at once.

1 tablespoon coarse
sea salt or kosher salt

1½ lb (750 g) cooked
fresh lobster meat, or 5 frozen
lobster tails, thawed and
halved lengthwise

2½ tablespoons
Champagne vinegar

2 teaspoons fresh
lemon juice

3½ tablespoons olive oil

½ teaspoon fine sea salt

½ teaspoon freshly
ground pepper

2 teaspoons minced
fresh tarragon

2 cups (2 oz/60 g) mixed
greens such as baby arugula
(rocket), watercress leaves,
and field greens

½ cup (½ oz/15 g) fresh
herbs such as whole tarragon
leaves, flat-leaf (Italian)
parsley leaves, and small
chervil sprigs

SERVES 8–10

PAN-SEARED SEA BASS WITH HERB BUTTER

When a dollop of herb butter is placed on a hot sea bass fillet, it melts immediately, infusing the fish with its flavor. Here, chives, fresh flat-leaf parsley, and chervil are used, but you can mix any fresh herb or a combination of herbs into butter. Dill and lemon verbena are other herbs that are commonly paired with fish.

To make the herb butter, cut the butter into slices 1 inch (2.5 cm) thick and put in a bowl. Add the chives, parsley, and chervil and mash with a fork or the back of a wooden spoon until evenly blended. Pack the butter tightly into a ramekin just large enough to hold it. Cover the ramekin with plastic wrap and refrigerate until ready to serve. (The herb butter can be made up to 2 days in advance; bring to room temperature before serving.)

Season the fish fillets with salt and pepper. Heat the oil in a large skillet over medium-high heat. Add the fillets and cook until lightly golden on the outside and opaque in the center, about 4 minutes per side.

Transfer the fillets to individual plates and top each with a tablespoon of the herb butter. Serve at once.

Flavored butters

In addition to herbs, try mixing other fresh elements into butter to create a rich and flavorful topping for fish or meat. Combinations to try include garlic and basil, rosemary and shallot, chile powder and lime zest, nasturtiums and sea salt, and tarragon and Dijon mustard.

Herb Butter

1/2 cup (4 oz/125 g) unsalted butter, at room temperature

1 teaspoon minced fresh chives

1 teaspoon minced fresh flat-leaf (Italian) parsley

1 teaspoon minced fresh chervil

6–8 sea bass or halibut fillets or steaks, each about 6 oz (185 g) and 1 inch (2.5 cm) thick

1 teaspoon sea salt

1 teaspoon freshly ground pepper

2 tablespoons extra-virgin olive oil

SERVES 6–8

GRILLED TOMATILLO CHICKEN FAJITAS

Mexican crema, a thin cultured cream, can be found at Mexican food stores and some supermarkets. Sour cream thinned with half-and-half (half cream) can be substituted. For a casual Mexican-themed dinner, set up the ingredients for the fajitas so guests can make their own. Serve with Mexican beer and margaritas (page 89).

To make the tomatillo salsa, position a rack 4 inches (10 cm) from the heat source and preheat the broiler (grill). Put the tomatillos, chiles, garlic, and onion on a rimmed baking sheet. Sprinkle with the cumin, oregano, and salt. Drizzle with the olive oil and toss to combine. Broil (grill), turning once, until the vegetables are soft and lightly charred, about 8 minutes. Let cool to room temperature, then transfer to a food processor and add the lime juice and cilantro. Using the pulse button, purée until almost smooth. Cover and refrigerate until ready to use or for up to 2 days.

Arrange the chicken breasts in a single layer in a shallow baking dish and sprinkle with the salt and pepper. Pour 1 cup (8 fl oz/250 ml) of the salsa over the chicken breasts, coating them evenly. Cover and refrigerate for at least 2 hours or up to 1 day. Transfer the remaining salsa to a small serving bowl, cover, and refrigerate until ready to serve.

Prepare a charcoal or gas grill for direct grilling over medium-high heat. Oil the grill rack and position it about 6 inches (15 cm) from the heat source. Rub the bell pepper halves and green onions with the olive oil.

Grill the bell pepper halves and green onions, turning frequently, until tender and lightly charred, 5–6 minutes for the peppers and 2–3 minutes for the onions. Slice the peppers into thin strips and cut the onions on the diagonal into 2-inch (5-cm) pieces. Wrap in aluminum foil to keep warm.

Remove the chicken from the marinade, discarding the marinade. Grill, turning once, until opaque throughout, about 20 minutes total. Cut the chicken on the diagonal into slices ½ inch (12 mm) thick, capturing any juices.

Arrange the chicken, bell peppers, and green onions on a warmed platter. Drizzle with any carving juices, the crema, and a little of the reserved salsa. Serve accompanied by the tortillas and salsa.

Roasted Tomatillo Salsa

1 lb (500 g) tomatillos, husks removed, rinsed and quartered

2 jalapeño chiles, seeded and coarsely chopped

2 cloves garlic

1 small white onion, quartered

1 teaspoon ground cumin

1 teaspoon dried oregano

½ teaspoon kosher salt

2 tablespoons olive oil

Juice of 2 limes

⅓ cup (⅓ oz/10 g) fresh cilantro (fresh coriander) leaves

3 lb (1.5 kg) boneless, skinless chicken breasts

1 teaspoon kosher salt

1 teaspoon pepper

2 each red and yellow bell peppers (capsicums), halved, seeded, and stemmed

6 green (spring) onions, roots and green tops trimmed

3 tablespoons olive oil

½ cup (4 fl oz/125 ml) Mexican crema

12 flour tortillas, 8 inches (20 cm) in diameter, warmed

SERVES 10–12

GRILLED SAUSAGES AND PORTOBELLOS

Precooked sausages made from beef, pork, lamb, or poultry and flavored with a variety of seasonings are sold in the meat department of many markets. A selection of three or four different kinds is perfect for a crowd. For vegetarians, offer grilled portobello mushrooms and red onions. Provide guests with freshly grilled rolls and a selection of condiments to assemble their own sandwiches.

Prepare a charcoal or gas grill for direct grilling over medium heat. Lightly brush the sausages and cut sides of the ciabatta rolls with ¼ cup (2 fl oz/60 ml) of the olive oil. Grill the sausages, turning once, until heated through and slightly charred, about 4 minutes on each side. Transfer the sausages to a cutting board.

In a bowl, whisk together the remaining ½ cup (4 fl oz/125 ml) olive oil, the balsamic vinegar, garlic, and thyme. Season to taste with salt and pepper. Brush the mushroom caps and onion slices with the olive oil mixture, coating them evenly. Grill the mushrooms and onions, turning once, until they are soft and lightly charred,

about 3 minutes on each side. Place the ciabatta rolls cut side down on the grate and grill until lightly toasted and warm, about 2 minutes.

While the vegetables and rolls are on the grill, cut the sausages on the diagonal into thirds. Capture any carving juices, if possible. Arrange the sausage pieces on a warmed serving platter. Drizzle any carving juices over the sausages. Arrange the mushrooms and onions alongside the sausages or on another warmed platter, and garnish with rosemary sprigs, if desired. Serve at once, with the ciabatta rolls and condiments.

5 lb (2.5 kg) assorted precooked sausages, at room temperature

10 ciabatta rolls, split in half

¾ cup (6 fl oz/180 ml) olive oil

¼ cup (2 fl oz/60 ml) balsamic vinegar

1 clove garlic, finely chopped

1 tablespoon fresh thyme leaves

Coarse salt and freshly ground pepper

10 portobello mushrooms, 5 inches (13 cm) in diameter, brushed clean and stems removed

3 red onions, sliced ¼ inch (6 mm) thick

Assorted condiments such as pickle relish, tomato relish, onion jam, pesto, crumbled fresh goat cheese, flavored mustards and mayonnaises, and sliced tomatoes

Fresh rosemary sprigs for garnish (optional)

SERVES 10

BEEF SKEWERS WITH SPICY PEANUT DIPPING SAUCE

This versatile dipping sauce, laden with fresh herbs and thickened with peanut butter, is uncommonly delicious. If you make the sauce and skewers in advance, plan to remove both from the refrigerator 30 minutes before cooking and serving, so that the meat cooks evenly and the sauce is creamy.

To make the marinade, stir together the sesame oil, vinegar, soy sauce, ginger, and green curry paste in a shallow baking dish. Set aside.

Trim the narrow end pieces off the flank steak, so that you are left with a rectangular piece. Wrap in plastic wrap and place flat in the freezer for 30 minutes. (This will facilitate the slicing of the meat.) Slice the steak against the grain on the diagonal into 36 slices, each ¼ inch (6 mm) wide. Add the steak to the marinade and cover with plastic wrap. Refrigerate for at least 30 minutes or up to 1 day.

To make the dipping sauce, in a food processor, combine the basil, cilantro, mint, chile, garlic, fish sauce, lime juice, and peanut butter and process until smooth. Transfer to a small serving bowl, cover with plastic wrap, and refrigerate until 30 minutes before serving. (The dipping sauce can be made up to 1 day in advance.)

Soak 36 wooden skewers in water to cover in a shallow baking dish for 30 minutes and then drain. Position a rack 6 inches (15 cm) from the heat source and preheat the broiler (grill).

Remove the beef slices from the marinade and drain well. Weave 1 slice of beef onto each skewer. Place the skewers on rimmed baking sheets, spacing them evenly. (The beef can be skewered 1 day in advance and stored in the refrigerator. Bring to room temperature before continuing.)

Broil (grill), turning once, until cooked through, about 4 minutes total.

To serve, place the bowl of dipping sauce and the skewers on a large platter. Sprinkle the green onions and peanuts over the skewers. Serve at once.

Marinade

⅓ cup (3 fl oz/80 ml) Asian sesame oil

2 tablespoons rice vinegar

2 tablespoons soy sauce

1 tablespoon peeled and grated fresh ginger

2 teaspoons Thai-style green curry paste

2-lb (1-kg) piece flank steak

Dipping Sauce

1 cup (1½ oz/45 g) tightly packed fresh basil leaves

1 cup (1½ oz/45 g) tightly packed fresh cilantro (fresh coriander) leaves

1 cup (1½ oz/45 g) tightly packed fresh mint leaves

1 serrano chile, seeded

2 cloves garlic

3 tablespoons Thai fish sauce

3 tablespoons fresh lime juice

½ cup (5 oz/155 g) chunky peanut butter

3 green (spring) onions, including tender green tops, thinly sliced on the diagonal

¼ cup (1½ oz/45 g) chopped dry-roasted peanuts

MAKES 36 SKEWERS;
SERVES 10–12

LAMB BROCHETTES WITH MINT GREMOLATA

Make up a few extra vegetable brochettes if you know some of your guests don't eat meat. Always place the vegetable brochettes around the perimeter of the grill where the temperature is lower, so that they are done at the same time as the meat brochettes.

To make the gremolata, in a small bowl, mix together the mint, parsley, garlic, and lemon zest until well blended. Cover and refrigerate until ready to use. (The gremolata can be prepared up to 4 hours in advance.)

Cut the lamb into 1¼-inch (3-cm) cubes. In a small bowl, whisk together the olive oil, wine, tomato paste, vinegar, rosemary, garlic, salt, and pepper until well blended. Put the lamb cubes in a large heavy-duty resealable plastic bag. Put the zucchini, eggplant, and onion pieces in another bag. Divide the marinade evenly between the 2 bags. Press out any excess air, seal the bags, turn to coat the contents evenly with the marinade, and refrigerate. The lamb can marinate overnight, but the vegetables should not marinate for more than 4 hours.

Strip the leaves off each rosemary branch, leaving a few leaves on the tip. Using a sharp knife, shape the other end to a sharp point. Soak the branches or skewers in water to cover in a shallow baking dish for 30 minutes and then drain. Prepare a charcoal or gas grill for direct grilling over medium-high heat. Oil the grill rack and position it about 6 inches (15 cm) from the heat source.

Remove the lamb pieces from the marinade and discard the marinade. Thread onto 8 of the rosemary branches, making sure not to crowd them so they cook evenly. Thread the vegetables in an alternating pattern onto the remaining 8 rosemary branches. Reserve the vegetable marinade for basting. Place the lamb skewers in the center of the grill over the hottest part of the fire and the vegetable skewers around them. Grill, turning and basting every few minutes, until the lamb is cooked through and the vegetables are tender and lightly charred, 10–12 minutes.

Arrange the skewers on a warmed platter, sprinkle with the mint gremolata, and serve.

Mint Gremolata

2 tablespoons chopped fresh mint

2 tablespoons chopped fresh flat-leaf (Italian) parsley

2 cloves garlic, minced

1 tablespoon grated lemon zest

2-lb (1-kg) piece trimmed boneless leg of lamb

1 cup (8 fl oz/250 ml) olive oil

½ cup (4 fl oz/125 ml) dry red wine

2 tablespoons tomato paste

2 tablespoons balsamic vinegar

3 tablespoons chopped fresh rosemary

2 cloves garlic, minced

2 teaspoons kosher salt

1 teaspoon ground pepper

2 each green and yellow zucchini (courgettes), cut into rounds 1 inch (2.5 cm) thick

2 slender eggplants (aubergines), cut into rounds 1 inch (2.5 cm) thick

2 large red onions, cut into 2-inch (5-cm) pieces

16 sturdy woody rosemary branches or wooden skewers

MAKES 16 SKEWERS; SERVES 8

ROASTED POTATO SALAD WITH GREEN ONION DRESSING

Preheat the oven to 400°F (200°C). Put the potatoes on a rimmed baking sheet, drizzle with the olive oil, sprinkle with the salt, and toss to coat evenly. Roast, tossing every 15 minutes, until the skins are crisp and golden brown, about 45 minutes. Let cool.

Meanwhile, make the dressing: In a food processor or blender, combine the cilantro leaves, green onions, garlic, sour cream, mayonnaise, vinegar, and mustard and process until smooth. Season to taste with salt and pepper, cover, and refrigerate until ready to use. (The dressing can be prepared up to 1 day in advance and refrigerated.)

To serve, put the cooled potatoes in a serving bowl, add the dressing, and toss to coat. Garnish with the cilantro sprigs. Serve at once, or cover and refrigerate for up to 4 hours.

3 lb (1.5 kg) baby Yukon gold potatoes, each about 1 inch (2.5 cm) in diameter

3 tablespoons olive oil

1 tablespoon kosher salt

Dressing

1/2 cup (1/2 oz/15 g) fresh cilantro (fresh coriander) leaves, plus sprigs for garnish

3 green (spring) onions, including tender green tops, chopped

1 clove garlic, chopped

1/2 cup (4 oz/125 g) sour cream

1/4 cup (2 fl oz/60 ml) mayonnaise

4 teaspoons red wine vinegar

4 teaspoons Dijon mustard

Kosher salt and freshly ground pepper

SERVES 10–12

GRILLED CORN WITH CHIPOTLE BUTTER

Corn becomes special when rubbed with seasoned butter, grilled in its husks, and spritzed with lime. Season the corn up to a day before grilling so it will have time to absorb the smoky flavor of the chipotle butter.

In a bowl, using a wooden spoon, mix the butter, chile powder, lime zest, and salt into a smooth paste. Set aside at room temperature for 30 minutes to blend the flavors.

Working with 1 ear of corn at a time, peel down the husks and remove the silk strands, making sure that the husks remain attached at the base of the ear. Using a pastry brush or small rubber spatula, brush or spread 1 tablespoon of the chipotle butter evenly over the ear of corn. Fold the husks back up over the ear so that it is completely enclosed. Repeat with the remaining ears of corn. (The corn can be prepared up to 1 day in advance.

Cover with plastic wrap and refrigerate, then bring to room temperature before grilling.)

Prepare a charcoal or gas grill for direct grilling over medium-high heat. Position a grill rack about 6 inches (15 cm) from the heat source.

Grill the ears of corn, turning often so that they cook evenly, until the kernels are tender and the husks are charred all over, 10–15 minutes. Arrange the corn on a platter with the lime quarters on top. Let each guest unwrap an ear of corn and squeeze a little lime juice over it before eating.

¾ cup (6 oz/185 g) unsalted butter, at room temperature

1 tablespoon chipotle chile powder

Grated zest of 2 limes

2 teaspoons kosher salt

12 ears of corn, husks intact

3 limes, quartered

SERVES 12

GRILLED ZUCCHINI AND FAVA BEANS

Use a quality salt to bring out the flavor of grilled vegetables. Sea salt is best, preferably *fleur de sel*, harvested along the Brittany coast of France. Look for a selection of sea salts at specialty-food stores.

Prepare a charcoal or gas grill for direct grilling over medium-high heat. Position a grill rack about 6 inches (15 cm) from the heat source.

Rub the fava bean pods and zucchini slices with the olive oil and season with the 1 teaspoon salt and the ½ teaspoon pepper. Arrange on the grill rack and grill, turning often, until

evenly charred and the zucchini slices are tender, about 5 minutes.

Transfer to a warmed platter, drizzle with olive oil, and sprinkle with salt and pepper. Allow guests to remove the favas from their pods and then squeeze the beans from their tough skins.

16 young, tender fava (broad) bean pods

3 medium zucchini (courgettes), trimmed and sliced lengthwise ½–1 inch (12 mm–2.5 cm) thick

3 tablespoons olive oil, plus more for drizzling

1 teaspoon sea salt, plus more for serving

½ teaspoon ground pepper, plus more for serving

SERVES 4

RATATOUILLE

Ratatouille, first popular in Provence, is the essence of summer. Juicy, just-picked tomatoes are essential because their juice forms the basis of the zesty sauce, and the mildly acidic tang they impart is a hallmark of a good ratatouille. Making this dish a day in advance allows the flavors time to blend and develop.

Bring a large saucepan of water to a boil. Using a slotted spoon, dip the tomatoes in the water for 30 seconds, then place in a colander. When the tomatoes are cool enough to handle, peel off the skins with your fingers or a knife. Coarsely chop the tomatoes, reserving the juice. Set aside.

In a large saucepan over medium-high heat, warm the olive oil. Add the onion and sauté until translucent, 3–4 minutes. Add the garlic and sauté for 1 minute. Add the eggplant and sauté until it has absorbed the oil, about 2 minutes. Add the tomatoes, zucchini, bell peppers, thyme, salt, and pepper and stir well.

Cook uncovered, stirring occasionally, until the eggplant is easily pierced with a fork, the other vegetables are soft, and the tomatoes have been reduced by one-third to one-half, about 45 minutes. Remove from the heat and stir in the basil.

Transfer to a serving bowl. Serve hot or at room temperature. (Ratatouille can be prepared up to 1 day in advance and refrigerated. Bring to room temperature or reheat and then add the chopped basil before serving.)

6 very ripe tomatoes, about 3 lb (1.5 kg) total weight

2 tablespoons extra-virgin olive oil

¼ cup (1½ oz/45 g) chopped yellow onion

6 cloves garlic, minced

1 large eggplant (aubergine), cut into 1-inch (2.5-cm) cubes

3 zucchini (courgettes), cut into slices ½ inch (12 mm) thick

2 red bell peppers (capsicums), seeded and cut into 1-inch (2.5-cm) pieces

2 teaspoons fresh thyme leaves

1 teaspoon salt

1 teaspoon freshly ground pepper

2 teaspoons finely shredded basil

SERVES 6–8

APRICOT-PISTACHIO TART

You can quickly assemble this delicious seasonal fruit tart using store-bought pastry dough and fruit preserves. For a fall variation, use 1/2 cup (5 oz/155 g) cranberry preserves instead of apricot, and substitute walnuts and poached pear halves for the pistachios and apricots.

Remove 1 sheet of puff pastry from the package and thaw in the refrigerator for 24–36 hours, or according to package directions. Wrap the remaining sheet in plastic wrap and keep frozen for another use.

Preheat the oven to 400°F (200°C). Lightly butter a 10-inch (25-cm) tart pan with a removable bottom.

On a lightly floured work surface, roll out the puff pastry sheet into an 11-inch (28-cm) square. Drape the dough over the rolling pin and transfer it to the prepared tart pan. Trim off the corners and then gather any overhang and press it into the sides of the pan to form a rim that is even in thickness. Using a fork, prick the bottom and sides of the dough. Place the tart shell in the freezer for 15 minutes. Remove from the freezer and bake the unfilled tart shell until lightly golden, about 15 minutes. Let cool.

While the tart shell is baking, in a bowl, toss the apricot halves together with the sugar and orange liqueur. Let stand to macerate at room temperature for 15 minutes.

To assemble the tart, spread the apricot preserves evenly over the bottom of the partially baked tart shell. Sprinkle the cinnamon, cardamom, and 4 tablespoons (1 oz/30 g) of the pistachios over the preserves. Arrange the apricot halves, cut sides down, in concentric circles over the preserves, and drizzle any of the juices remaining in the bowl over the surface. Sprinkle the remaining 2 tablespoons pistachios over the top.

Bake the tart until the apricots are tender and the pastry is golden brown, 30–40 minutes. Remove from the oven and drizzle the honey over the top. Let cool on a wire rack before slicing. (The tart can be prepared up to 4 hours in advance, cooled, tented with aluminum foil, and stored at room temperature.)

1 package (17 oz/530 g) frozen puff pastry

10 apricots, halved and pitted

2 tablespoons sugar

1 tablespoon orange liqueur

1/2 cup (5 oz/155 g) thick apricot preserves

1 teaspoon ground cinnamon

1/2 teaspoon ground cardamom

6 tablespoons (1 1/2 oz/45 g) chopped pistachios

2 tablespoons honey

SERVES 8

FOLD-UP BLUEBERRY AND RASPBERRY TARTS

These rustic fruit tarts are sublime when berries are at their seasonal peak. Other types of berries, like strawberries or blackberries, can be used. Or, you can substitute 3 cups (18 oz/560 g) thinly sliced peaches, nectarines, or plums, or a mixture, keeping in mind complementary flavors and colors.

Preheat the oven to 375°F (190°C). Have ready 2 ungreased rimmed baking sheets.

Place 1 pastry dough round on a baking sheet. In a large bowl, combine the blueberries, raspberries, sugar, and lemon juice and stir carefully to mix. Place half of the fruit in the center of the pastry round and gently spread to within 2 inches (5 cm) of the edge. Dot the fruit with half of the butter. Fold the uncovered edges of the pastry over the fruit, covering as much of the fruit as possible and pleating, pinching, and folding the dough as necessary.

Repeat with the second baking sheet and pastry round and the remaining fruit and butter.

Bake until the pastry is golden brown and the fruit is bubbling, about 30 minutes. Let cool on the pans on wire racks for 10–15 minutes. Cut into wedges and serve.

Add a finishing touch

For a crisp, sugar-crusted edge, brush egg white over the pastry and sprinkle with coarse sugar just before baking. Serve with vanilla ice cream or lightly whipped cream.

2 rolls store-bought pie pastry dough, each about 13 inches (33 cm) in diameter and 1/4 inch (6 mm) thick, thawed if frozen

1 1/2 cups (6 oz/185 g) blueberries

1 1/2 cups (6 oz/185 g) raspberries

1/3 cup (3 oz/90 g) sugar

2 teaspoons fresh lemon juice

2 tablespoons cold unsalted butter, cut into small pieces

SERVES 12–14

ICE CREAM SUNDAES

Transfer the store-bought sauces to squirt bottles and label each bottle. Place the blueberries, raspberries, maraschino cherries, chocolate chips, toffee-bar pieces, cookies, and nuts in small bowls for toppings. Transfer the whipped cream to a small serving bowl.

Arrange the whipped cream and ice creams on ice so that they remain cold, and place within easy reach of guests. Set out the sauces, toppings, bananas, and waffle cones. Let guests create their own ice cream confections.

Setting up a sundae bar

To create a self-service backyard sundae bar, you'll need the following equipment: plenty of ice in sturdy tubs to keep ice cream and whipped cream cold; plastic squirt bottles for the sauces; ice cream scoops; small bowls for toppings; and ice cream bowls and spoons.

1½ cups (12 fl oz/375 ml) chocolate sauce

1½ cups (12 fl oz/375 ml) caramel sauce

1½ cups (12 fl oz/375 ml) strawberry sauce

2 cups (8 oz/250 g) blueberries

2 cups (8 oz/250 g) raspberries

1 cup (6 oz/185 g) maraschino cherries

1 cup (6 oz/185 g) miniature chocolate chips

1 cup (5 oz/155 g) broken toffee-bar pieces

1 cup (3 oz/90 g) whole miniature cookies or cookie pieces

1 cup (4 oz/125 g) walnuts or sliced (flaked) almonds, toasted

2 cups (16 fl oz/500 ml) heavy (double) cream, whipped

1 qt (32 fl oz/1 l) vanilla ice cream

1 qt (32 fl oz/1 l) chocolate ice cream

1 qt (32 fl oz/1 l) strawberry ice cream

3 bananas, unpeeled

12 waffle ice cream cones

SERVES 10–12

GRILLED PEACHES WITH TOASTED ALMONDS

Grilling caramelizes the natural sugars present in the flesh of fruit, intensifying its flavor and subtle sweetness. Peaches are an especially good choice for grilling, but you can also try nectarines, apricots, Pluots, plums, or figs with similar results. Clean the grill rack well to make sure no other flavor is imparted to the fruit.

Preheat the oven to 350°F (180°C). Spread the almonds in a single layer on a baking sheet. Place in the oven and toast, stirring once or twice, until fragrant and dark brown, about 15 minutes. Remove from the oven, carefully transfer to a cutting board, and let cool. Coarsely chop and set aside. (The almonds can be toasted up to 2 days in advance and stored in an airtight container.)

Prepare a charcoal or gas grill for direct grilling over high heat. Lightly oil the grill rack and position it 6 inches (15 cm) from the heat source.

Lightly brush the peach halves all over with the olive oil. Place, round side down, on the grill rack and grill until grill marks appear, about 2 minutes. Using tongs, turn and grill again until grill marks appear on the cut side and the peaches are warmed through, about 4 minutes longer.

Place 2 halves on each plate, spoon on a little cream, and sprinkle with some of the almonds. Serve at once.

Grilled fruit galore

Grilled stone fruits make a wonderful light summer dessert when accompanied by ice cream or whipped cream. They have myriad other uses as well. Try pairing them with a creamy cheese in salads or with crostini. Some nice combinations include grilled plums and fresh goat cheese; grilled apricots and ricotta; or grilled figs and Gorgonzola.

½ cup (2½ oz/75 g) almonds

6–8 ripe yellow peaches, halved and pitted

2 teaspoons extra-virgin olive oil

½ cup (4 fl oz/125 ml) heavy (double) cream, lightly whipped

SERVES 6–8

CAPPUCCINO GRANITA

Simple and elegant, this refreshing granita should be made at least 12 hours ahead so that the ice crystals are frozen solid. It makes a light and flavorful dessert for a warm summer evening. Serve with store-bought amaretto cookies in their decorative wrapping papers or squares of dark chocolate.

In a large bowl, combine the coffee, sugar, and cinnamon and stir until the sugar is dissolved. Whisk in ¼ cup (2 fl oz/60 ml) of the cream and chill for about 30 minutes. Pour the mixture into a shallow gratin dish and place in the freezer. Using a fork, scrape around the sides of the dish every 30 minutes to break up the ice crystals until all the liquid is completely frozen, about 3 hours. Cover tightly with plastic wrap and keep frozen until ready to serve. (The granita can be prepared up to 2 days in advance and stored in the freezer.)

Just before serving, using a handheld mixer, whip the remaining 1 cup (8 fl oz/250 ml) cream on medium-high speed until soft peaks form, about 3 minutes. Divide the granita between 8 coffee cups with saucers. Top each cup with a dollop of whipped cream and a sprinkle of chocolate shavings. Place an amaretto cookie alongside each cup and serve at once.

Serving cappuccino granita

Granita looks lovely in small glass bowls or cups that showcase the ice crystals; cappuccino cups and tall, thin glasses also work well. Garnish this granita with whipped cream, chocolate shavings, or a sprinkling of sweetened cocoa powder, ground cinnamon, or freshly grated nutmeg.

4 cups (32 fl oz/1 l) freshly brewed double-strength coffee

½ cup (4 oz/125 g) sugar

2 teaspoons ground cinnamon

1¼ cups (10 fl oz/310 ml) heavy (double) cream

Semisweet (plain) chocolate shavings for garnish

8 store-bought amaretto cookies in wrappers for serving

SERVES 8

PLUM GRATIN WITH HONEY-LAVENDER CREAM

The thickened lavender-infused cream recalls the flavor of honey-lavender ice cream, a specialty of Provence. The sweetness of the honey and the richness of the cream marry well with the tart plums. You can substitute any stone fruit—such as apricots or Pluots—for the plums.

Preheat the oven to 425°F (220°C). Generously butter a 9-inch (23-cm) round or oval flameproof dish. Sprinkle 3 tablespoons of the sugar over the bottom.

Cut the plums in half and remove the pits. Cut each half into slices ½ inch (12 mm) thick. Put the slices in the prepared dish, arranging them snugly in a single layer of concentric circles. In a bowl, using a whisk, beat the eggs until lemon yellow, about 30 seconds. Beat in the milk, flour, and salt to make a smooth batter. Pour evenly over the plums. Sprinkle with the remaining 5 tablespoons (3 oz/90 g) sugar and the almonds. Dot with the butter.

Bake the gratin until the batter is puffed and golden, the butter and sugar have formed a crust, and the plums have softened, about 15 minutes. If necessary, place under the broiler (grill) to finish browning the crust.

Meanwhile, make the honey-lavender cream: In a small saucepan over high heat, combine the cream, honey, and lavender and bring to a boil. Cook, stirring, until the cream has reduced by about one-third, about 5 minutes. Remove from the heat and set aside to cool. Strain the cooled cream through a fine-mesh sieve placed over a small bowl. (The cream can be made up to 1 day in advance and refrigerated. Bring to room temperature before serving.)

To serve, spoon the warm gratin into small dessert bowls and drizzle the honey-lavender cream over each serving.

½ cup (4 oz/125 g) sugar

4 or 5 large plums

2 large eggs

½ cup (4 fl oz/125 ml) whole milk

½ cup (2½ oz/75 g) all-purpose (plain) flour

⅛ teaspoon salt

⅓ cup (2 oz/60 g) coarsely chopped almonds

2 tablespoons unsalted butter, cut into small pieces

Honey-Lavender Cream

⅔ cup (5 fl oz/160 ml) heavy (double) cream

1 tablespoon plus 1 teaspoon lavender or wildflower honey

1 teaspoon pesticide-free fresh or dried lavender blossoms without stems, crushed

SERVES 6–8

SAUTÉED CHERRIES OVER CHOCOLATE-CHUNK ICE CREAM

In a nonreactive bowl, toss together the cherries and lemon juice. Set aside.

In a large frying pan over medium heat, melt the butter. Add the cherries and brown sugar and sauté until the cherries are soft and the sugar is caramelized, about 5 minutes. Remove from the heat and swirl in the kirsch.

To serve, scoop the ice cream into individual bowls or stemmed glasses. Top each serving with an equal amount of the warm cherries and drizzle some of the pan juices over the top. Serve at once.

2 cups (12 oz/375 g) pitted cherries

Juice of 1/2 lemon

1/4 cup (2 oz/60 g) unsalted butter

1/4 cup (2 oz/60 g) firmly packed light brown sugar

2 tablespoons kirsch

1 pt (16 fl oz/500 ml) chocolate-chunk ice cream

SERVES 4

ITALIAN ICE CREAM TREATS

To make the gelato easier to scoop, remove from the freezer about 10 minutes before serving to soften slightly. Using a small ice cream scoop (about 1 3/4 inches/4.5 cm across) or a sturdy tablespoon, fill each cone or small glass with a scoop of gelato. If you have small ice cream spoons, stand a spoon in the side of each scoop. Garnish with a tuile cookie or chopped fresh fruit, if using. Serve at once.

1/2 gallon (2 l) chocolate, vanilla, strawberry, or pistachio gelato or lemon, lime, mango, or raspberry sorbet, or a combination

16–20 mini ice cream cones (optional)

16–20 store-bought tuile cookies or wafers for garnish (optional)

Chopped fruit for garnish (optional)

SERVES 8–10

autumn

drinks and starters

PEAR SPARKLERS 153

SPICED APPLE CIDER WITH CLOVE ORANGES 153

WHITE GRAPE SPLASH 154

KIR 154

GRAPEFRUIT MARTINIS 157

CRANBERRY GIN FIZZ 157

GORGONZOLA BRUSCHETTA WITH FIGS 160

FIGS WRAPPED IN PROSCIUTTO 160

CROSTINI WITH ARTICHOKE-PARMESAN SPREAD 163

SPICED NUTS 163

DATES STUFFED WITH PARMESAN
SLIVERS AND WALNUTS 164

ROASTED ALMOND AND DATE SPREAD 164

ANTIPASTO PLATTER 167

BAKED BRIE WITH PISTACHIOS AND DRIED FRUIT 168

ROASTED WALNUTS 168

soups and salads

WHITE BEAN SOUP WITH ESCAROLE 171

BUTTERNUT SQUASH SOUP 172

MÂCHE, RADISH, AND SUGARED PECAN SALAD 175

CELERY, PEAR, AND TOASTED HAZELNUT SALAD 176

ARUGULA SALAD WITH PECORINO AND PINE NUTS 179

MIXED GREEN SALAD WITH CROSTINI 179

APPLE AND FENNEL SLAW 180

TUNA AND FARRO SALAD 183

mains and sides

GRILLED HALIBUT WITH POTATO-FENNEL PURÉE 184

SQUASH RAVIOLI WITH BROWN BUTTER AND PECANS 187

HERBED PORK TENDERLOIN WITH PANCETTA
AND CAPERS 188

BLACK-PEPPER BEEF TENDERLOIN WITH CELERY ROOT 191

ROAST TURKEY WITH PAN GRAVY 192

BUTTERFLIED TURKEY WITH HERB GLAZE AND GRAVY 195

FRESH CRANBERRY RELISH 196

MASHED BUTTERNUT SQUASH WITH
SAGE AND BUTTER 196

MASHED YUKON GOLD POTATOES 199

GREEN BEANS WITH GARLIC 200

CARROTS GLAZED WITH MUSTARD
AND BROWN SUGAR 200

APPLE, CELERY, AND SOURDOUGH STUFFING 203

WILD RICE AND LEEK PILAF 204

COLLARD GREENS PIQUANT 204

BROCCOLI AND BLUE CHEESE GRATIN 207

BRUSSELS SPROUTS WITH PANCETTA AND ONIONS 208

desserts

APPLE-PEAR CRISP 211

APPLE AND CRANBERRY GALETTE 212

PEAR TART TATIN WITH BRANDIED CREAM 215

PECAN PRALINE PIE 216

PUMPKIN CHEESECAKE 219

CHOCOLATE-HAZELNUT BROWNIES WITH ICE CREAM 220

PEAR SPARKLERS

Place ice cubes in tall glasses. Add about
3 tablespoons pear juice to each glass, and then
pour in about ½ cup (4 fl oz/125 ml) sparkling
water. Slice the pear into thin wedges to garnish
each glass, then serve at once.

Ice cubes

1½–2 cups (12–16 fl oz/
375–500 ml) bottled
pear juice

4–5 cups (32–40 fl oz/
1–1.25 l) sparkling
water, chilled

1 Anjou pear for garnish

SERVES 8–10

SPICED APPLE CIDER
WITH CLOVE ORANGES

Stud each orange with 12 cloves. Place the oranges
in a large pot, pour in the apple cider, and set over
low heat. Tie the 4 cinnamon sticks and the star
anise in a cheesecloth (muslin) bundle and add
it to the pot. Bring to a simmer and keep warm
over low heat until serving. To serve, ladle into
cups and garnish each serving with a cinnamon
stick tied with orange zest.

3 small oranges or
tangerines, about ¾ lb
(375 g) total weight

36 whole cloves

3 qt (3 l) apple cider

4 cinnamon sticks, plus
10–12 sticks each tied
with an orange zest strip

2 whole star anise

SERVES 10–12

WHITE GRAPE SPLASH

Select 4 tumblers or wineglasses. Put several ice cubes and 6 frozen grapes in each glass. Pour ¾ cup (6 fl oz/180 ml) of the grape juice into each glass, then top with about ¼ cup (2 fl oz/60 ml) of the sparkling water. Garnish with a mint sprig and serve at once.

Ice cubes

24 red or green grapes, frozen

3 cups (24 fl oz/750 ml) white grape juice

1 cup (8 fl oz/250 ml) sparkling water, chilled

Fresh mint sprigs for garnish

SERVES 4

KIR

Chill 4 tumblers or wineglasses. Pour 2 teaspoons of the crème de cassis into each glass and top with about ⅔ cup (5 fl oz/160 ml) of the wine. Garnish with a lemon twist and serve at once.

8 teaspoons crème de cassis

2½ cups (20 fl oz/625 ml) dry white wine such as Sauvignon Blanc, chilled

4 long, narrow lemon twists for garnish

SERVES 4

GRAPEFRUIT MARTINIS

Grapefruit vodka, or any citrus-flavored vodka, makes for a fresh flavored and vibrant martini. The Cointreau, replacing the usual vermouth, intensifies the citrus taste, and the raspberry juice adds a pink hue. For a festive occasion, sugar the rim.

Select 8 martini glasses. Pour the sugar onto a small plate. Rub the rim of each glass with the large grapefruit wedge, then dip the rim in the sugar. Put the glasses in the freezer to chill for at least 30 minutes.

Fill a cocktail shaker half full with ice and add half each of the vodka, Cointreau, and raspberry juice. Cover with the lid and shake for 20 seconds. Strain into 4 of the glasses and add a grapefruit segment to each glass. Repeat to make 4 more martinis. Serve at once.

Flavorful rims

Add a sweet or savory flourish to a cocktail by rimming the glass with sugar or salt. Sugar on its own pairs nicely with a fruity martini or a Cosmopolitan; mix in cinnamon for a winter or apple-flavored cocktail. With a Bloody Mary, try celery salt. Finely grated citrus zest mixed with salt makes a terrific flavor combination for a tequila-based drink, such as a margarita.

¼ cup (2 oz/60 g) superfine (caster) sugar

1 large Ruby Red or pink grapefruit wedge, plus 8 segments

Ice cubes

2 cups (16 fl oz/500 ml) Ruby Red grapefruit vodka

¼ cup (2 fl oz/60 ml) Cointreau

1½ teaspoons raspberry juice

SERVES 8

CRANBERRY GIN FIZZ

A dash of tart cranberry juice gives the gin fizz a colorful update for fall. If fresh cranberries are in season, add a few to each drink for a garnish, along with a slice of lemon or orange. Serve these cocktails at Thanksgiving, alongside bowls of spiced nuts.

Select 8 small glasses and put 2 or 3 ice cubes in each glass. Fill a cocktail shaker half full with ice and add half each of the lemon juice, gin, sugar, and cranberry juice. Cover with the lid and shake for 20 seconds. Strain into 4 of the glasses. Add 2 tablespoons club soda to each glass, stir, and garnish with the lemon slices. Repeat to make 4 more drinks. Serve at once.

Festive drinks for holiday fare

A sparkling cocktail sets the tone for any celebration, and you can use any fresh fruit as a base. Cranberry juice makes a deliciously tart base for a bracing cocktail. For a colorful garnish, float a few fresh cranberries in each drink, thread some on a toothpick, or freeze them in ice cubes. Pomegranates, blood oranges, and grapes are other great choices for sprucing up holiday drinks.

16–24 ice cubes

½ cup (4 fl oz/125 ml) fresh lemon juice (3–4 lemons)

2 cups (16 fl oz/500 ml) gin

2½ tablespoons superfine (caster) sugar

1 cup (8 fl oz/250 ml) unsweetened cranberry juice

½ cup (4 fl oz/125 ml) club soda

Lemon slices for garnish

SERVES 8

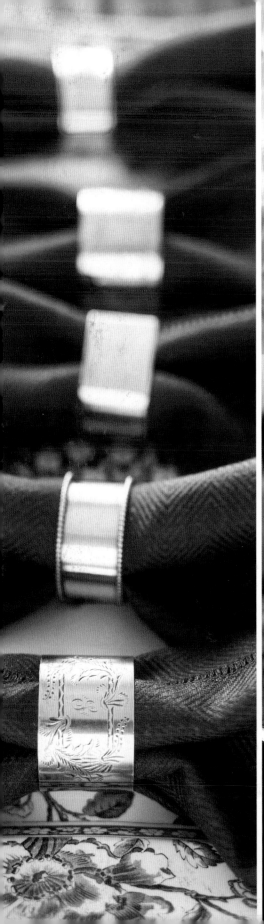

GORGONZOLA BRUSCHETTA WITH FIGS

Prepare a charcoal or gas grill for direct grilling over high heat. Lightly oil the grill rack and position it 6 inches (15 cm) from the heat source.

Drizzle one side of the baguette slices with the olive oil and place, coated side down, on the grill rack. Grill until lightly golden, 3–4 minutes. Turn and grill until the second side is dry, about 1 minute longer. Remove from the grill. (The baguette slices can be grilled up to 1 day in advance.)

Spread each slice with about 1 tablespoon of the Gorgonzola and top with about 1 tablespoon of the chopped figs. Place fig leaves, if using, on a platter and arrange the bruschetta on top. Serve at once.

20 baguette slices, ¼ inch (6 mm) thick (about 1 baguette)

2 tablespoons extra-virgin olive oil

½ lb (250 g) Gorgonzola cheese, at room temperature

10–12 ripe, soft figs, coarsely chopped

Fig leaves for garnish, optional

SERVES 6–8

FIGS WRAPPED IN PROSCIUTTO

Using a sharp knife, cut the prosciutto slices lengthwise into strips 1 inch (2.5 cm) wide. Trim off the tough stem end of the figs and cut each fig in half lengthwise. Wrap each fig half with a strip of prosciutto and place, cut side up, on a tray or platter. (The figs can be prepared up to 2 hours in advance, covered, and refrigerated; bring to room temperature before serving.)

½ lb (250 g) thinly sliced prosciutto

18–24 soft, ripe figs, 1½–2 lb (750 g–1 kg) total weight

SERVES 12–14

CROSTINI WITH ARTICHOKE-PARMESAN SPREAD

Keep jars of artichoke hearts on hand in the pantry for this tasty and easy Italian-style spread. Make sure to drain and dry the artichokes well so the flavors of the spread are not diluted.

Preheat the oven to 350°F (180°C). Arrange the baguette slices in a single layer on a baking sheet. Bake, turning once halfway through baking, until lightly golden, about 25 minutes total. Remove from the oven and let cool.

Drain the artichoke hearts, rinse briefly, pat dry, and coarsely chop. In a food processor, combine the artichoke hearts, butter, cheese, pepper, and lemon juice. Purée until smooth. Season to taste with salt.

Evenly spread the purée on the baguette slices. Arrange the crostini on a platter, garnish with the chopped basil, and serve.

30 baguette slices, ¼ inch (6 mm) thick (about 1 large baguette)

1 jar (12 oz/375 g) water-packed artichoke hearts

1½ tablespoons unsalted butter, at room temperature

¾ cup (3 oz/90 g) freshly grated Parmesan cheese

¼ teaspoon freshly ground pepper

2 teaspoons fresh lemon juice

Salt

Finely chopped fresh basil for garnish

SERVES 8–10

SPICED NUTS

The combination of salt and spice makes these seasoned nuts a hit with cocktails. Try mixing different nuts and adding other flavors such as cumin, or nut oils such as walnut or almond. The spiced nuts can be made a week ahead and stored in an airtight container.

Preheat the oven to 350°F (180°C).

In a bowl, combine the nuts, olive oil, salt, sugar, paprika, and cayenne and mix well. Spread the nuts in a single layer on a rimmed baking sheet. Toast, stirring several times, until the nuts are fragrant and have taken on color, about 10 minutes. Transfer to paper towels and let cool, then transfer to a bowl. Garnish with the rosemary and serve.

1 lb (500 g) mixed shelled nuts such as almonds, walnuts, cashews, and pistachios

2 tablespoons extra-virgin olive oil

1 tablespoon sea salt

1 teaspoon sugar

2 teaspoons sweet paprika

½ teaspoon cayenne pepper

Rosemary leaves for garnish

SERVES 8–10

DATES STUFFED WITH PARMESAN SLIVERS AND WALNUTS

With a paring knife, make a small lengthwise incision in each date and carefully remove the pits.

Using a vegetable peeler, shave the cheese into ribbons. Tuck some cheese and a walnut half into the slit in each date. Arrange on a platter and serve.

24 large dates, preferably Medjool

2-oz (60-g) piece Parmesan cheese

24 walnut halves

SERVES 8–10

ROASTED ALMOND AND DATE SPREAD

In a food processor, combine the almonds, dates, Madeira, and orange zest. Pulse until the almonds are finely ground and the mixture is almost smooth. (The spread can be prepared up to this point, transferred to a container, covered, and refrigerated for up to 1 week. Bring to room temperature before serving.)

When ready to serve, transfer the spread to a small serving bowl. Set the bowl alongside a selection of cheeses and breads.

1/2 cup (2 1/2 oz/75 g) unsalted roasted whole almonds

1 package (8 oz/250 g) pitted dates

1/4 cup (2 fl oz/60 ml) Madeira or dry sherry

Zest of 1 orange

SERVES 8

ANTIPASTO PLATTER

Antipasto plates are a festive and easy way to serve a crowd. Buy 1 lb (500 g) each mixed olives and assorted Italian cured meats (such as coppa, soppressata, and salami) and some bread sticks. Arrange the olives and meats on 1 large or 2 smaller platters, leaving room for the mozzarella and mushroom appetizers below.

To make the pancetta with mozzarella, preheat the broiler (grill). Wrap each bocconcino with a strip of pancetta and secure the strips with toothpicks. Place on a baking sheet, slip under the broiler 4 inches (10 cm) from the heat source, and broil (grill) until the pancetta starts to crisp and the cheese is warmed through but not melted, about 4 minutes. Transfer to the platter and serve hot or warm.

To make the stuffed mushrooms, preheat the oven to 350°F (180°C). Remove the mushroom stems, making a cavity in the caps. Set the caps aside. Using a sharp paring knife, trim and discard the bottom ¼ inch (6 mm) of the stems. Mince the remaining stems and set aside. Finely chop 6 of the prosciutto slices. Cut the remaining 2 slices into strips about ½ inch (12 mm) wide, then cut again into strips about 1½ inches (4 cm) long. Set aside.

In a frying pan over medium heat, melt the butter. Add the minced mushroom stems and shallots and sauté until the shallots are translucent, about 1 minute. Add the chopped prosciutto and sauté for about 30 seconds. Remove from the heat and mix in the cheese, bread crumbs, and minced parsley. Brush the mushroom caps with the olive oil, then stuff each cap with an equal amount of the cheese mixture and place in a greased baking dish.

Bake until the mushrooms are tender and the stuffing is browned, 20–25 minutes. Let cool in the baking dish on a wire rack. To serve, roll up the prosciutto strips, place a strip on each cap, top with a parsley leaf, and arrange on the platter with the mozzarella balls.

Pancetta with Mozzarella

1 container (12 oz/375 g) bocconcini (small mozzarella balls) or ½ lb (250 g) mozzarella cheese, cut into 1-inch (2.5-cm) cubes

⅓ lb (155 g) thinly sliced pancetta, cut into strips about 2 inches (5 cm) long and 1 inch (2.5 cm) wide

Prosciutto-Stuffed Mushrooms

24 medium-size mushrooms such as button or cremini

8 thin slices prosciutto, fat trimmed

4 tablespoons (2 oz/60 g) unsalted butter

⅓ cup (2 oz/60 g) minced shallots

3 oz (90 g) soft goat cheese

⅓ cup (⅔ oz/20 g) fresh bread crumbs

2 tablespoons minced fresh flat-leaf (Italian) parsley, plus leaves for garnish

1 tablespoon extra-virgin olive oil

SERVES 8–10

BAKED BRIE WITH PISTACHIOS AND DRIED FRUIT

Soft, warm Brie—jeweled with pistachio nuts, dried apricots, and cranberries—is delicious spread on crackers or toasted baguette slices. The cooking time will vary depending on the ripeness of your cheese.

Preheat the oven to 350°F (180°C).

Place the cheese round on a rimmed baking sheet. Prick the top with a fork in a dozen places and drizzle with 1½ teaspoons of the brandy. In a bowl, toss the remaining brandy with the apricots, cranberries, and pistachios. Scatter the fruit mixture evenly over the top of the round. Bake until the cheese warms and softens, 8–10 minutes. Using a wide spatula, transfer the round to a plate lined with lettuce leaves. Serve with baguette slices or crackers.

1 round Brie cheese (1 lb/500 g)

2 tablespoons Cognac or orange-flavored brandy

⅓ cup (2 oz/60 g) dried apricots, cut into thin strips

3 tablespoons dried cranberries or golden raisins (sultanas)

3 tablespoons pistachios

Lettuce leaves for serving

Toasted thin baguette slices or crackers

SERVES 10–12

ROASTED WALNUTS

Both sweet and savory, these spiced walnuts are great to have on hand when guests arrive. You can prepare them well in advance. Stored in an airtight container at room temperature, they will keep for up to 3 weeks.

Preheat the oven to 375°F (190°C). Line a rimmed baking sheet with aluminum foil and lightly butter the foil.

In a small bowl, combine the sugar, cinnamon, cardamom, cloves, salt, and pepper. In a medium bowl, whisk the egg white until frothy. Add the sugar mixture and whisk to blend. Whisk in the orange zest. Add the walnuts and stir until thoroughly coated. Spread the coated walnuts on the prepared pan in an even layer. Bake the nuts, stirring every 10 minutes to separate them, until golden, about 30 minutes. Transfer to a bowl and let cool. Store in an airtight container for up to 3 weeks.

3 tablespoons sugar

2 teaspoons ground cinnamon

½ teaspoon ground cardamom

½ teaspoon ground cloves

¼ teaspoon fine sea salt

¼ teaspoon freshly ground pepper

1 large egg white

2 teaspoons grated orange zest

2 cups (8 oz/250 g) walnut halves

SERVES 10–12

WHITE BEAN SOUP WITH ESCAROLE

This hearty soup, full of the simple flavors of beans, broth, and greens, can be enjoyed by the cup or bowl. Offer guests freshly grated Parmesan cheese to sprinkle over the top and slices of warm crusty bread for dipping. If you can't find escarole, you can use one bunch of Swiss chard, the stems removed and leaves shredded.

Pour 8 qt (8 l) water into a large pot, add the beans and the 1 tablespoon salt, then bring to a boil over medium-high heat. Reduce the heat to low, cover partially, and simmer until the beans are tender to the bite, 2–2½ hours. Using a slotted spoon, transfer the beans to a bowl and set aside, reserving the cooking liquid in the pot. You should have about 8 cups (64 fl oz/2 l) liquid remaining. Return the bean broth to a gentle boil over medium-high heat and cook until reduced to about 4 cups (32 fl oz/1 l), about 10 minutes.

Hold the escarole to make a tight bunch. Using a sharp knife, cut the escarole crosswise into strips ¼ inch (6 mm) wide, then chop coarsely. Set aside.

In a clean pot over medium heat, warm the olive oil. When the oil is hot, add the onions and sauté until translucent, 3–4 minutes. Add the escarole and cook, stirring, until it wilts, 2–3 minutes. Add the chicken stock, the reduced bean cooking liquid, the pepper, the 1 teaspoon salt, and the bay leaves. Bring to a boil over high heat. Reduce the heat to low and simmer, uncovered, until the flavors are blended, about 30 minutes. Stir in the beans and cook for 5 minutes longer.

Taste and adjust the seasoning. Serve hot, garnished with the Parmesan cheese.

2¼ cups (16 oz/500 g) dried cannellini, white kidney, flageolet, or small lima beans

1 tablespoon plus 1 teaspoon coarse sea salt or kosher salt

1½ heads escarole (Batavian endive)

3 tablespoons extra-virgin olive oil

1½ small yellow onions, minced

8 cups (64 fl oz/2 l) chicken stock or reduced-sodium chicken broth

1 teaspoon freshly ground pepper

2 bay leaves

¾ cup (3 oz/90 g) grated Parmesan cheese

SERVES 12–14

BUTTERNUT SQUASH SOUP

The subtle sweetness of apple or pear lends an elegant nuance to this creamy autumnal soup. Roasting the fruit and vegetables first gives them a rich, caramelized taste. Plan to make the soup a day in advance to allow the flavors to mingle; reheat and add the sage butter garnish just before serving.

Preheat the oven to 450°F (230°C). Line a rimmed baking sheet with aluminum foil.

In a small bowl, stir together the oil and vinegar. Brush the cut sides of the squash, the apple halves, and the onions with the oil mixture. Place the squash and apple halves, cut side down, and the onions on the prepared baking sheet. Bake, turning the fruit and vegetables twice, until tender and lightly browned, about 30 minutes for the apple and 45–50 minutes for the vegetables. Transfer to a cutting board and let cool. Scoop out the flesh from the squash halves, discarding the peel. Coarsely chop the apple and onions.

Transfer the squash flesh, onions, and apple to a large saucepan and add the stock and nutmeg.

Bring to a boil over medium-high heat and then reduce the heat to medium. Simmer until very tender, about 20 minutes. Remove from the heat and let cool. In a blender, purée the soup in batches until smooth. Return the soup to the pan, stir in the half-and-half, season to taste with salt and pepper, and heat through over medium heat. (The soup can be prepared up to 2 days in advance and stored, tightly covered, in the refrigerator.)

Just before serving, melt the butter in a small frying pan over medium heat. Add the sage and sauté until the butter browns lightly and the sage is crisp. Ladle the soup into warmed bowls and garnish with the sage butter.

3 tablespoons canola oil

2 tablespoons balsamic vinegar

2 butternut squashes, about 3 lb (1.5 kg) total weight, halved lengthwise and seeded

1 large Granny Smith apple or Anjou or Bosc pear, peeled, halved, and cored

2 yellow onions, quartered

6 cups (48 fl oz/1.5 l) chicken stock or reduced-sodium chicken broth

1/4 teaspoon freshly grated nutmeg

Salt and freshly ground pepper

1/2 cup (4 fl oz/125 ml) half-and-half (half cream) or 1/2 cup (4 oz/125 g) plain yogurt

1 tablespoon unsalted butter

1/4 cup (1/3 oz/10 g) chopped fresh sage

SERVES 8–10

MÂCHE, RADISH, AND SUGARED PECAN SALAD

Mâche is a tender, nutty-flavored salad leaf that is sold in ready-to-use bags in the produce section of many supermarkets. For a substitute, use a mixture of tender arugula (rocket) and baby spinach leaves. Crumbled goat cheese can be substituted for the blue cheese. Try to cut the radishes as thinly as possible—if you own a mandoline, it will come in handy here.

To prepare the pecans, preheat the oven to 350°F (180°C). Rinse the pecans in a sieve and set aside to drain. In a small bowl, combine the sugar, dry mustard, and cayenne and mix well. Add the pecans and toss until evenly coated. Spread the pecans on a nonstick rimmed baking sheet and toast in the oven until dark brown, about 10 minutes. Transfer the pecans to a plate, let cool, and set aside.

To make the vinaigrette, in a small bowl, whisk together the shallot, olive oil, vinegar, and Dijon mustard. Season to taste with salt and black pepper. Let stand at room temperature for at least 30 minutes or up to 4 hours.

To serve, combine the mâche and radish slices in a salad bowl. Drizzle with the vinaigrette and toss until evenly coated. Top with the blue cheese and the pecans. Serve at once.

Candied nuts in salads

Nuts roasted with sugar and spices are the perfect addition to salads of all kinds: the sugar cuts through vinegary dressing, and the crunchiness adds texture. You can prepare these pecans up to 1 week in advance. Store them in an airtight container at room temperature. Walnut halves can be used in place of the pecans.

Sugared Pecans

½ cup (2 oz/60 g) pecan halves

1 teaspoon sugar

¼ teaspoon dry mustard

Pinch of cayenne pepper

Vinaigrette

1 shallot, finely chopped

⅓ cup (3 fl oz/80 ml) olive oil

2 tablespoons red wine vinegar

1 teaspoon Dijon mustard

Kosher salt and freshly ground black pepper

1 package (4 oz/125 g) mâche

8 radishes, thinly sliced

¼ lb (125 g) blue cheese, crumbled

SERVES 4

CELERY, PEAR, AND TOASTED HAZELNUT SALAD

This crunchy and refreshing salad is best in autumn, when many varieties of pears are available. Removing the strings from the celery stalks ensures a tender base for this composed seasonal salad. Walnuts and walnut oil can be substituted for the hazelnuts and hazelnut oil.

Preheat the oven to 350°F (180°C).

To remove the strings from the celery, hold each stalk, large end up, and pull the strings downward by trapping them between your fingers and the blade of a paring knife. Using a chef's knife or a mandoline, cut the celery into slices ⅛ inch (3 mm) thick. Cut the leaves into small pieces. Put all the celery in a bowl of ice water and set aside. (The celery can be prepared up to 1 day in advance and refrigerated.)

Spread the hazelnuts in a single layer on a baking sheet. Bake, stirring once or twice, until the skins start to darken and wrinkle, 12–15 minutes. Remove from the oven. When the nuts are cool enough to handle, wrap in a kitchen towel and rub vigorously to remove the skins. Some specks of skin will remain. Coarsely chop the nuts and set aside.

In a large bowl, combine the hazelnut oil, vinegar, salt, and pepper and mix well with a fork. Drain the celery and pat dry with a paper towel. Add to the bowl and turn to coat with the vinaigrette.

Cut each pear in half lengthwise. Using a spoon, scoop out the seeds and the fibers surrounding them, as well as the fibers that run down the center from the stem. Cut lengthwise into slices ½ inch (12 mm) thick. Set aside.

Using a slotted spoon, remove the celery from the vinaigrette and divide among chilled salad plates. Arrange the pear slices on top and drizzle with the vinaigrette. Sprinkle with the chopped nuts and serve at once.

8–10 celery stalks

Ice water

½ cup (2½ oz/75 g) hazelnuts (filberts)

2½ tablespoons hazelnut oil

1 tablespoon white balsamic vinegar or pear vinegar

¼ teaspoon salt

¼ teaspoon freshly ground white pepper

4 ripe pears such as Bosc or Bartlett, peeled

SERVES 6–8

ARUGULA SALAD WITH PECORINO AND PINE NUTS

In a small frying pan over medium heat, toast the pine nuts, shaking the pan gently, until lightly golden, 2–3 minutes. Transfer to a plate and set aside.

In a large salad bowl, combine the olive oil, vinegars, salt, and pepper and mix well with a fork or whisk. Add the arugula and toss to coat evenly.

Divide the arugula among individual chilled salad plates. Using a vegetable peeler, shave the cheese into thin ribbons and divide among the salads. Sprinkle with the pine nuts and serve at once.

3 tablespoons pine nuts

3 tablespoons extra-virgin olive oil

1 tablespoon balsamic vinegar

1 teaspoon red wine vinegar

1/2 teaspoon each sea salt and freshly ground pepper

4–5 cups (4–5 oz/125–155 g) baby arugula (rocket)

2 oz (60 g) pecorino cheese

SERVES 4–6

MIXED GREEN SALAD WITH CROSTINI

To make the vinaigrette, in a small bowl, whisk together the olive oil, lemon juice, and shallot. Season to taste with salt and pepper. (The vinaigrette can be prepared in advance, covered, and kept at room temperature for up to 4 hours.)

Remove the tough, fibrous exterior leaves from the escarole and discard. Tear the interior leaves into bite-sized pieces.

In a large bowl, combine the escarole and mâche. Whisk the vinaigrette, drizzle it over the greens, and toss to coat the leaves well. Arrange the crostini around the perimeter of the bowl. To serve, divide the salad greens among individual plates and accompany each serving with 2 crostini.

1/4 cup (2 fl oz/60 ml) extra-virgin olive oil

2 tablespoons fresh lemon juice

1 shallot, minced

Coarse salt and freshly ground pepper

1 head escarole (Batavian endive)

1 bag (10 oz/315 g) mâche

8 store-bought toasted baguette crostini or cheese crisps

SERVES 4

APPLE AND FENNEL SLAW

Chilling the apples, fennel, and cabbage in ice water before dressing them keeps them crunchy and helps to retain their individual flavors. The fennel is blanched to tenderize it and chilled again for crunch. Golden raisins complement the tart, sweet dressing. Substitute buttermilk for the whole milk to add extra zing.

Slice the cut face of each cabbage half into paper-thin slices. Place the sliced cabbage in a large bowl and add ice water to cover. Set aside.

Fill another large bowl with ice water and squeeze the juice of ½ lemon into it. Bring a large saucepan three-fourths full of water to a boil over high heat and add the juice of the remaining lemon half. Cut off the stems and feathery fronds of the fennel bulbs and remove any bruised or discolored outer leaves. Working with 1 fennel bulb at a time, cut the bulb in half lengthwise and cut out any tough core parts. Using a sharp knife or the small julienne blade of a mandoline, slice each half into matchsticks and place immediately in the bowl of lemon water. Repeat with the remaining fennel bulbs. When all the fennel is cut, transfer with a slotted spoon to the boiling water and blanch for 30 seconds. (Reserve the bowl of water and lemon for the apples.) Drain the blanched fennel and rinse well under cold running water. Transfer to a fresh bowl of ice water. Set aside.

Working with 1 apple at a time, quarter it and cut away the core. Starting with the rounded side, slice each quarter into matchsticks and place immediately in the reserved lemon water. Repeat with the remaining apples.

In another bowl, combine the mayonnaise, sugar, lemon juice, vinegar, milk, and salt and mix well. Taste and adjust the seasoning and consistency. The dressing should be both sweet and tangy, and the consistency should be pourable, not thick. Add a little more milk if the dressing is too thick.

Drain the cabbage, pat dry, and place in a large bowl. Drain the fennel, squeeze gently to remove excess water, pat dry, and add to the bowl of cabbage. Drain the apples, pat dry, and add to the bowl. Add the raisins, green onions, and parsley. Add the dressing and mix well. Cover and refrigerate until ready to serve.

1 head green cabbage, halved and cored

Ice water as needed

1 lemon, halved

4 fennel bulbs

4 Granny Smith apples

1 cup (8 fl oz/250 ml) mayonnaise

¼ cup (2 oz/60 g) sugar

¼ cup (2 fl oz/60 ml) fresh lemon juice

¼ cup (2 fl oz/60 ml) sherry vinegar

2 tablespoons whole milk, or more if needed

1 teaspoon salt

1 cup (6 oz/185 g) golden raisins (sultanas)

4 green (spring) onions, including tender green parts, thinly sliced

½ cup (¾ oz/20 g) minced fresh flat-leaf (Italian) parsley

SERVES 12–14

TUNA AND FARRO SALAD

Farro, an ancient wheat that is similar to spelt and is a specialty of Tuscany and Umbria, makes an excellent salad because it maintains its shape and texture. It is sold in Italian specialty-food stores and health-food markets. Whole-wheat (wholemeal) couscous or short-grain brown rice makes a good substitute.

In a large saucepan over high heat, combine the farro with 6 cups (48 fl oz/1.5 l) water and bring to a boil. Reduce the heat to medium-low, cover, and simmer until the grains are tender but not soft, about 30 minutes. Pour into a colander, rinse with cold water, and set aside to drain.

To make the vinaigrette, in a large salad bowl, whisk together the olive oil, vinegar, lemon juice, peppercorns, and salt.

Add the farro, tuna, onion, celery, parsley, and garlic to the vinaigrette and toss until evenly coated. Season to taste with salt and pepper. (The salad can be prepared up to 4 hours in advance, covered with plastic wrap, and stored at cool room temperature.)

To serve, add the radicchio to the salad bowl and toss to combine. Garnish with the lemon wedges and drizzle with a little extra-virgin olive oil. Serve at once.

Italian family-style feast

For an Italian feast, serve this salad with Herbed Pork Tenderloin with Pancetta and Capers (page 188) and Roasted Cauliflower with Green Olives (page 283). Place each dish on a large platter and let diners help themselves at the table. Finish the meal off with Cappuccino Granita (page 140).

1 1/2 cups (10 1/2 oz/330 g) farro, soaked in water to cover for 20 minutes and drained

Vinaigrette

1/3 cup (3 fl oz/80 ml) olive oil

2 tablespoons red wine vinegar

2 tablespoons fresh lemon juice

4 teaspoons brine-cured green peppercorns, chopped

1/2 teaspoon kosher salt

1 can (10 1/2 oz/330 g) Italian tuna packed in olive oil, drained and flaked

1/2 white onion, finely diced

1 celery stalk, thinly sliced

1/3 cup (1/2 oz/15 g) coarsely chopped fresh flat-leaf (Italian) parsley

1 clove garlic, finely chopped

Kosher salt and freshly ground pepper

1 small head radicchio, julienned

Lemon wedges for garnish

Extra-virgin olive oil for drizzling

SERVES 8

GRILLED HALIBUT WITH POTATO-FENNEL PURÉE

Bulb fennel, also known as Florentine fennel or sweet anise, comes into season in early summer and is available well into the autumn months. Puréed with potatoes, it makes a light alternative to traditional mashed potatoes. The purée can be prepared up to 30 minutes before serving, covered, and reheated.

Brush the halibut fillets with the olive oil to coat completely. In a small bowl, stir together the chervil, fennel seeds, orange zest, salt, and pepper. Sprinkle the mixture over the halibut fillets, distributing it evenly so that all sides are seasoned. Transfer the fillets to a shallow baking dish, cover, and refrigerate for up to 4 hours. Bring to room temperature 15 minutes before grilling.

To make the potato-fennel purée, in a large pot over medium-high heat, warm the olive oil. Add the fennel and sauté until translucent and golden, about 15 minutes. Add the stock, potatoes, and 1 teaspoon salt. Reduce the heat to maintain a simmer, cover, and cook until the potatoes are soft when pierced with a knife, about 30 minutes.

Drain the potatoes and fennel in a colander, return to the pot, and immediately mash with a potato masher. Add the butter and slowly pour in the half-and-half while stirring with a wooden spoon. Add the mayonnaise and continue to stir until light and creamy. Season to taste with salt and pepper.

Prepare a charcoal or gas grill for direct grilling over medium-high heat. Lightly oil the grill rack and position it about 6 inches (15 cm) from the heat source.

Grill the halibut fillets, turning once, until opaque throughout, 3–4 minutes on each side. Garnish with chervil and serve at once with the purée alongside.

4 skinless halibut fillets, each about 6 oz (185 g) and 1 inch (2.5 cm) thick

¼ cup (2 fl oz/60 ml) olive oil

1 tablespoon chopped fresh chervil, plus extra for garnish

1 teaspoon fennel seeds, crushed

Grated zest of ½ orange

1 teaspoon kosher salt

½ teaspoon freshly ground pepper

Potato-Fennel Purée

2 tablespoons olive oil

2 fennel bulbs, quartered, cored, and finely diced

2½ cups (20 fl oz/625 ml) chicken stock or reduced-sodium chicken broth

2 lb (1 kg) Yukon gold potatoes, peeled and quartered

Kosher salt

2 tablespoons unsalted butter

½ cup (4 fl oz/125 ml) half-and-half (half cream), heated

2 tablespoons mayonnaise

Freshly ground pepper

SERVES 4

SQUASH RAVIOLI WITH BROWN BUTTER AND PECANS

Squash-filled ravioli is an autumn specialty in Italy. A simple topping of brown butter and pecans complements the flavor of the squash without overpowering it. If you have a pasta machine, it will make rolling the dough much faster and easier.

Preheat the oven to 375°F (190°C). To make the filling, rub the cut sides of the squash with the olive oil and place, cut side down, on a baking sheet. Bake until tender when pierced with a knife, 1–1½ hours. Let cool, scoop the flesh into a bowl, and mash with a fork. Mix in the egg, cheese, salt, and spices. Set aside. (The filling can be prepared up to 12 hours in advance and refrigerated.)

To make the pasta, in the bowl of a stand mixer fitted with the paddle attachment, whisk together the eggs and salt. With the mixer running on low speed, gradually add 2 cups flour, about ¼ cup (1½ oz/45 g) at a time, until most has been added and the dough forms a ball on the paddle. Pinch the dough. It should feel moist but not sticky and be fairly smooth. If not, beat in more flour as necessary. Knead the dough on a lightly floured surface until firm, smooth, and moist but not sticky, about 1 minute. Cover with an inverted bowl and let rest for at least 30 minutes or up to 2 hours.

Divide the dough in half. On a large, floured surface, roll out one half into a 16-by-20-inch (40-by-50-cm) rectangle about ⅛ inch (3 mm)

thick. Using a knife, lightly mark the dough into 1½-inch (4-cm) squares. Place 1 teaspoon filling in the center of each square. Roll out the remaining dough into a same-sized rectangle and lay it over the filling. Lightly press down on the mounds of filling, then press around each filling to seal. Using a pastry wheel or knife, cut along the length on both sides and across the top and bottom to make 1½-inch squares. Crimp the edges to seal. (The ravioli can be made up to 2 hours in advance. Place in a single layer on a floured kitchen towel, dust the tops with flour, and cover with another towel.)

Bring a large pot of water to a boil and add the salt. Working in batches, use a slotted spoon to slide the ravioli into the water. Reduce the heat to low and simmer until tender, 3–5 minutes. Using the spoon, transfer to a warmed platter.

Meanwhile, in a frying pan over medium-high heat, melt the butter. Add the pecans and cook, stirring, until the butter is golden, 2–3 minutes. Cool for 30 seconds, stir in the lemon juice, and pour over the ravioli. Garnish with the sage.

Filling

1 butternut squash,
2–2½ lb (1–1.25 kg),
halved lengthwise and
seeds discarded

1 teaspoon
extra-virgin olive oil

1 large egg, lightly beaten

½ cup (2 oz/60 g) finely
shredded Gruyère cheese

1 teaspoon salt

½ teaspoon ground cinnamon

½ teaspoon ground cloves

½ teaspoon freshly
ground pepper

Pasta Dough

3 large eggs

½ teaspoon salt

2–2¼ cups (10–11½ oz/
315–360 g) all-purpose
(plain) flour

2 teaspoons salt

½ cup (4 oz/125 g)
unsalted butter

¼ cup (1 oz/30 g) coarsely
chopped pecans

1 tablespoon fresh
lemon juice

6–8 fresh sage leaves
for garnish

SERVES 6–8

HERBED PORK TENDERLOIN WITH PANCETTA AND CAPERS

Saturated with the flavors of rosemary and sage, these pork tenderloins are a quick interpretation of the popular *porchetta* found throughout Tuscany and traditionally served at room temperature. Garnish the platter with fresh sage or rosemary sprigs. Use leftover pork in sandwiches or salads.

In a small bowl, combine the olive oil, rosemary, sage, fennel seeds, kosher salt, and pepper and mix well. Using the tip of a sharp paring knife, make 8 crosswise incisions ½ inch (12 mm) deep evenly spaced along the length of each tenderloin. Insert a garlic quarter into each incision. Rub the rosemary-sage mixture over the tenderloins. Wrap 2 slices of pancetta around each of the tenderloins in a spiral pattern. Place the tenderloins, side by side, in a baking dish. Cover tightly with plastic wrap and refrigerate for at least 24 hours or up to 2 days.

Remove the pork from the refrigerator and let stand at room temperature for 1 hour before roasting. Preheat the oven to 375°F (190°C).

Transfer the tenderloins to a small roasting pan and pat dry with paper towels. Roast until an instant-read thermometer inserted into the thickest part registers 150°F (65°C), about 30 minutes. Let cool. Remove the pancetta slices and finely chop them. Set aside. (The pork can be prepared up to this point 1 day in advance. Cover with plastic wrap and refrigerate along with the chopped pancetta. Bring to room temperature before serving.)

To fry the capers, in a bowl, toss the capers with the cornmeal until lightly coated. In a nonstick frying pan over high heat, warm the olive oil. When it is hot, drop in the capers and fry until golden, 1–2 minutes. Using a slotted spoon, transfer to a plate lined with a paper towel to drain. Lightly sprinkle the capers with sea salt.

To serve, thinly slice the pork and arrange on a serving platter. Scatter the fried capers and pancetta over the pork slices.

1 tablespoon olive oil

2 tablespoons chopped fresh rosemary

2 tablespoons chopped fresh sage

1 tablespoon fennel seeds, crushed

1½ teaspoons kosher salt

½ teaspoon freshly ground pepper

2 pork tenderloins, trimmed, about 1½ lb (750 g) total weight

4 cloves garlic, quartered lengthwise

4 thin slices pancetta

Fried Capers

¼ cup (2 oz/60 g) capers, drained and patted dry

1 tablespoon fine cornmeal

½ cup (4 fl oz/125 ml) olive oil

Sea salt

SERVES 8

BLACK-PEPPER BEEF TENDERLOIN WITH CELERY ROOT

Mashed celery root provides a seasonal alternative to potatoes as a partner to roast beef. Spiked with the tang of horseradish, the creamy purée makes an especially delicious companion. Round out the meal with Brussels Sprouts with Pancetta and Onions (page 208).

Preheat the oven to 450°F (230°C). Place a wire rack in a shallow roasting pan just large enough to hold the beef tenderloin. Rub the tenderloin all over with the olive oil, salt, and pepper.

Roast until an instant-read thermometer inserted into the thickest part of the beef registers 115°–120°F (46°–49°C) for rare, about 20 minutes; 125°–130°F (52°–54°C) for medium-rare, about 25 minutes; or 130°–140°F (54°–60°C) for medium, about 30 minutes. Transfer to a cutting board and tent with aluminum foil. Let the tenderloin rest for about 15 minutes.

While the tenderloin is roasting, prepare the celery root: Using a knife, remove the coarse brown skin. Rinse the celery root and then cut into 1-inch (2.5-cm) cubes. Put the cubes in a large saucepan and add water to cover by 3 inches (7.5 cm). Add the salt and bring to a boil over high heat. Reduce the heat to medium and cook until the cubes are tender when pierced

with a fork, about 15 minutes. Drain, return to the saucepan, and cover. (This can be done up to 2 hours in advance.)

About 10 minutes before serving, in a small saucepan over medium heat, combine the cream, milk, and butter and heat until steaming but not boiling, 2–3 minutes. Pour over the celery root. Using a potato masher or the back of a fork, mash the celery root until it forms a coarse purée. Stir in the horseradish, salt, and pepper. Taste and adjust the seasoning. Cover and keep warm.

Cut the beef into slices ½ inch (12 mm) thick. Spoon the celery root onto one side of a warmed serving platter and sprinkle with the celery root leaves. Arrange the beef slices on the other side of the platter and serve at once.

1 beef tenderloin,
2½–3 lb (1.25–1.5 kg)

2 tablespoons
extra-virgin olive oil

1½ teaspoons sea salt

1 tablespoon freshly
ground pepper

Celery Root

2½ lb (1.25 kg) celery root
(celeriac) (about 1 large root)

1 teaspoon sea salt

2 tablespoons heavy
(double) cream

2 tablespoons whole milk

3 tablespoons
unsalted butter

2 tablespoons prepared
horseradish

1 teaspoon sea salt

1 teaspoon freshly
ground pepper

Chopped celery root leaves
or celery leaves for garnish

SERVES 6–8

ROAST TURKEY WITH PAN GRAVY

There is nothing quite like the smell of a turkey roasting in the oven, and the eager anticipation of the feast that awaits. Instead of throwing out the neck and giblets, use them to create a rich stock, then incorporate it with the pan drippings for a flavorful pan gravy. Serve with Apple, Celery, and Sourdough Stuffing (page 203).

In a saucepan over low heat, combine the turkey neck and giblets, the whole onion, parsley, celery leaves, and 8 cups (64 fl oz/2 l) water and bring to a simmer. Season with salt and pepper, cover, and simmer for 1 hour. Strain through a fine-mesh sieve, discarding the solids. Cover and refrigerate until needed.

Meanwhile, position a rack in the lower third of the oven and preheat to 325°F (165°C). Season the turkey inside and out with salt and pepper and loosely stuff the neck and body cavities with the herb sprigs. Truss the turkey or tie the legs with kitchen string. Place breast side up on a rack in a roasting pan. Spread 2 tablespoons of the butter over the breast. In a small pan over low heat, melt the remaining 4 tablespoons (2 oz/60 g) butter; stir in the lemon zest and ¼ cup (2 fl oz/60 ml) water.

Roast the turkey, basting with the lemon butter every 20 minutes, until pan drippings have accumulated, then baste with the drippings. After 1½ hours, add the quartered onion and carrots to the pan and continue to roast, basting every 30 minutes. If the breast begins to overbrown, cover loosely with aluminum foil. Roast until an instant-read thermometer

inserted into the thickest part of the thigh away from the bone registers 175°F (80°C), 3½–4 hours total. Transfer the turkey to a cutting board, tent with aluminum foil, and let rest for 20 minutes before carving.

Meanwhile, skim off all but about 4 tablespoons (2 fl oz/60 ml) of the fat and juices in the pan, leaving the vegetables. Set the pan over medium heat and add 2 cups (16 fl oz/500 ml) of the stock, stirring to scrape up any browned bits. Stir over medium-high heat for 2 minutes, and then pour through a sieve set over a bowl, pressing on the solids. Use a large spoon to skim off the fat, then pour into a saucepan, add 4 cups (32 fl oz/1 l) of the stock (reserve the remainder for another use), and simmer briskly over medium-high heat for 5 minutes. Add the cornstarch mixture and stir until thickened, about 3 minutes. Stir in the Cognac, if using, and simmer for 1 minute.

Pour the gravy into a warmed gravy boat. Snip the string, carve the turkey, and arrange on a warmed platter. Serve with the gravy.

1 turkey, 18–20 lb (9–10 kg), neck and giblets removed and reserved, brought to room temperature (1½ hours)

2 yellow onions, 1 left whole and stuck with 2 whole cloves, 1 quartered

2 fresh flat-leaf (Italian) parsley sprigs

¼ cup (⅓ oz/10 g) celery leaves

Salt and freshly ground pepper

5 sprigs fresh sage, rosemary, or thyme, or a combination

6 tablespoons (3 oz/90 g) unsalted butter, at room temperature

1 tablespoon minced lemon zest

2 carrots, unpeeled, cut into 1-inch (2.5-cm) pieces

¼ cup (1 oz/30 g) cornstarch (cornflour) stirred into ¼ cup (2 fl oz/60 ml) water

¼ cup (2 fl oz/60 ml) Cognac (optional)

SERVES 10–12, WITH LEFTOVERS

BUTTERFLIED TURKEY WITH HERB GLAZE AND GRAVY

A butterflied turkey makes a handsome presentation, especially when wreathed with rosemary sprigs and lemons. Fresh herbs and garlic, rubbed both under and over the skin, infuse the bird with flavor. Use the leftover turkey (if there is any) to make sandwiches the next day.

Position the bird, breast side down, on a cutting board. Using kitchen shears or a large knife, cut along one side of the backbone until the bird is split open. Pull open the halves of the bird. Cut down the other side of the backbone to free it, then cut between the rib plates and remove any small pieces of bone. Turn the bird breast side up, opening it as flat as possible, and cover with a sheet of plastic wrap. Using a rolling pin or your hands, press it firmly to break the breastbone and flatten the bird. Season the bird with salt and pepper.

In a bowl, mix together the garlic, shallots, minced parsley, oregano, minced rosemary, mustard, lemon juice, and olive oil. Use your fingers to push some of the herb mixture under the skin of the breast and legs. Rub the remaining herb mixture over the surface of the bird. Place on a baking sheet, cover loosely with plastic wrap, and refrigerate for 6–24 hours. Bring the turkey to room temperature (about 1 hour) before roasting.

Meanwhile, in a saucepan over low heat, combine the turkey neck and giblets, the onion, parsley sprigs, celery leaves, and 6 cups (48 fl oz/1.5 l) water and bring to a simmer. Cover and cook for 1 hour, then strain, cover, and refrigerate the stock until ready to make the gravy.

Preheat the oven to 375°F (190°C). Spray a roasting pan with nonstick cooking spray and place a rack in the pan. Place the turkey, breast side up, on the rack, and tuck the legs in tightly. Brush with the melted butter. Roast until the skin is crisp and deep brown and an instant-read thermometer inserted into the thickest part of the thigh away from the bone registers 175°F (80°C), 2¼–2¾ hours. Transfer the turkey to a warmed serving platter, tent with aluminum foil, and let rest for 20 minutes.

After transferring the turkey to a platter, set the roasting pan on the stove top over medium-high heat. Add the wine, stirring to scrape up the browned bits on the pan bottom, and cook until the wine is reduced by half, about 10 minutes. Add 4 cups (32 fl oz/1 l) of the stock (reserve any remaining stock for another use) and bring to a boil. Stir in the dissolved cornstarch and cook until thickened, about 5 minutes.

Pour the gravy into a warmed gravy boat. Garnish the serving platter with the rosemary sprigs and lemon halves. Carve the turkey at the table and pass the gravy.

1 turkey, 12–14 lb (6–7 kg), neck and giblets removed and reserved

Salt and freshly ground pepper

6 cloves garlic, minced

¼ cup (1½ oz/45 g) minced shallots

⅓ cup (½ oz/15 g) minced fresh flat-leaf (Italian) parsley, plus 2 sprigs for stock

3 tablespoons minced fresh oregano

3 tablespoons minced fresh rosemary, plus sprigs for garnish

3 tablespoons Dijon mustard

3 tablespoons fresh lemon juice

3 tablespoons olive oil

1 yellow onion

¼ cup (⅓ oz/10 g) celery leaves

1–2 tablespoons unsalted butter, melted

1 cup (8 fl oz/250 ml) dry white wine

¼ cup (1 oz/30 g) cornstarch (cornflour) stirred into ¼ cup (2 fl oz/60 ml) water

4 lemons, halved

SERVES 8–10, WITH LEFTOVERS

FRESH CRANBERRY RELISH

This tangy-sweet condiment is quick to assemble in a food processor. Both the orange and apple are left unpeeled for extra texture and flavor. Prepare the relish up to 2 days before serving so that the flavors can blend.

Quarter the unpeeled orange and remove any seeds. Cut the orange into 1-inch (2.5-cm) pieces. Quarter and core the unpeeled apple and cut it into 1-inch (2.5-cm) chunks. In a food processor, combine the orange, apple, cranberries, sugar, and ginger. Process until finely minced. Transfer to an airtight container, cover, and store in the refrigerator for up to 2 weeks.

A lively accompaniment

Serve this tart, flavorful relish alongside roasted chicken, pork, or, of course, turkey at a Thanksgiving feast. It also makes a delicious spread for sandwiches made with the leftovers.

1 large orange

1 large tart apple such as Granny Smith

3 cups (12 oz/375 g) fresh cranberries

½ cup (4 oz/125 g) sugar

2 thin slices peeled fresh ginger

SERVES 10–12

MASHED BUTTERNUT SQUASH WITH SAGE AND BUTTER

Golden butternut squash whips up nicely for this tasty and colorful side dish. You can make this dish several hours ahead; before serving, reheat it in the oven at 325°F (165°C) for about 20 minutes.

Preheat the oven to 400°F (200°C). Lightly butter a rimmed baking sheet.

Place the squash halves, cut side down, on the prepared baking sheet. Bake until the squash is easily pierced with a fork, 40–50 minutes. Let cool slightly, then scoop out the flesh, discarding the peel, and transfer to a large bowl. Add the orange juice, half-and-half, sage, and 2 tablespoons of the butter. Season to taste with salt and pepper. Mash with a potato masher or beat with an electric mixer until blended and smooth. Transfer to a warmed serving bowl.

Just before serving, in a small saucepan over medium-high heat, melt the remaining 4 tablespoons (2 oz/60 g) butter and cook until it turns golden brown, about 3 minutes. Drizzle the butter over the squash. Serve hot.

2 butternut squashes, about 4 lb (2 kg) total weight, halved lengthwise and seeded

½ cup (4 fl oz/125 ml) fresh orange juice

½ cup (4 fl oz/125 ml) half-and-half (half cream)

½ teaspoon chopped fresh sage

6 tablespoons (3 oz/90 g) unsalted butter

Salt and freshly ground pepper

SERVES 10–12

MASHED YUKON GOLD POTATOES

With their golden color and buttery flavor, Yukon gold potatoes are excellent mashed with a zesty addition of garlic and fresh chives. A quick sauté softens the heat of garlic to a gentle sweetness. You can make the mashed potatoes up to 2 hours in advance. Reheat them in the top pan of a double boiler over simmering water.

Put the potatoes in a large pot and add water to cover. Salt the water, bring to a boil over medium heat, and then reduce the heat to medium-low. Cover and simmer, stirring once or twice, until the potatoes are tender when pierced with a fork, about 30 minutes. Drain, reserving about ½ cup (4 fl oz/125 ml) of the cooking liquid.

While the potatoes are cooking, in a small saucepan over low heat, melt 2 tablespoons of the butter. Add the garlic and sauté just until it turns opaque, 1–2 minutes. Do not let it brown. Set aside.

Pour the milk into a small saucepan. Place over medium-low heat and gently bring to a simmer. Set aside and keep warm.

Return the potatoes to the pot and place over low heat. Mash thoroughly with a potato masher. Using a wooden spoon, gradually stir in ¾ cup (6 fl oz/180 ml) of the hot milk, the remaining 4 tablespoons (2 oz/60 g) butter, the sautéed garlic, and the chives. Add the remaining milk and, if necessary, the reserved cooking liquid, adding just enough for the desired consistency. Stir until light and fluffy. Do not overmix or the potatoes will turn gummy. Season to taste with salt and pepper. Serve hot.

5 lb (2.5 kg) Yukon gold potatoes, peeled and cut into large chunks

Salt

6 tablespoons (3 oz/90 g) unsalted butter, at room temperature

12 large cloves garlic, minced

1½ cups (12 fl oz/375 ml) whole milk

½ cup (¾ oz/20 g) minced fresh chives

Freshly ground pepper

SERVES 10–12

GREEN BEANS WITH GARLIC

Trim the stem ends of the beans in advance and have the beans ready for quick cooking. You may also blanch the beans ahead and sauté them with the garlic just before serving. You want the beans to be tender-crisp and not too soft.

Have ready a large bowl of ice water. Bring a large pot three-fourths full of water to a boil. Salt the water, add the green beans, and cook until tender-crisp, 4–5 minutes. Drain, transfer immediately to the ice water, and let cool for 1 minute. Drain again and pat dry.

In a large frying pan over medium heat, melt the butter. Add the garlic and cook, stirring, just until pale gold, 2–3 minutes. Add the beans and tarragon and toss to coat with the garlic butter.

Season to taste with salt and pepper. Cover partially and cook, stirring occasionally, until the beans are heated through, 3–4 minutes. Top with Parmesan shavings just before serving. Serve hot.

Pass the green beans

Sautéed green beans are an ideal side dish for nearly any meal, especially fish or roasted poultry. If serving with fish, omit the Parmesan cheese and add a squeeze of fresh lemon juice or some grated lemon zest before serving.

Salt

2 lb (1 kg) small, slender green beans, stem ends trimmed

¼ cup (2 oz/60 g) unsalted butter

4 cloves garlic, minced

2 teaspoons minced fresh tarragon, or ½ teaspoon dried tarragon

Freshly ground pepper

3-oz (90-g) piece Parmesan or grana padano cheese, shaved with a vegetable peeler (about ¾ cup)

SERVES 10–12

CARROTS GLAZED WITH MUSTARD AND BROWN SUGAR

Brown sugar caramelized with butter and Dijon mustard creates a sweet-hot glaze for carrots. Garnish with a sprinkling of fresh chives to add color and flavor.

Peel the carrots then slice on the diagonal. Bring a saucepan three-fourths full of water to a boil. Salt the water, add the carrots, and cook until tender, 6–8 minutes. Drain well.

Return the pan of carrots to medium heat. Add the butter, mustard, and brown sugar, season to

taste with salt and pepper, and stir gently to coat. Cook, stirring constantly, until the carrots are evenly glazed. Transfer to a warmed serving bowl and sprinkle with the chives. Serve hot.

8 large carrots

Salt

1 tablespoon unsalted butter

1 tablespoon Dijon mustard

1 tablespoon firmly packed light brown sugar

Freshly ground pepper

⅓ cup (½ oz/15 g) coarsely chopped fresh chives

SERVES 8–10

APPLE, CELERY, AND SOURDOUGH STUFFING

The sweet-tart character of Granny Smith apples combines with the tang of sourdough bread in this moist, flavorful stuffing. The crusts add a nice chewiness, but if you prefer, you may cut them off. Whether stuffed inside the bird or baked on its own, this is a welcome accompaniment to roasted turkey or chicken.

Preheat the oven to 250°F (120°C). Spread the bread cubes on 2 rimmed baking sheets and dry in the oven for 40 minutes. Remove from the oven and set aside. Raise the oven temperature to 375°F (190°C).

In a large frying pan over medium heat, melt 3 tablespoons of the butter. Add the onions and celery and sauté until soft, about 10 minutes. Transfer to a large bowl. In the same frying pan, melt another 2 tablespoons of the butter, add the apples, and sauté until glazed, about 5 minutes. Transfer to the bowl holding the onion-celery mixture. Add the sage, thyme, nutmeg, salt to taste, and the pepper and mix well. Again in the same frying pan, melt the remaining 7 tablespoons butter, add the bread cubes and parsley, and toss to coat. Transfer to the bowl.

In another bowl, combine the eggs and stock and whisk until blended. Pour the stock mixture over the bread mixture and toss gently.

Transfer the stuffing to a lightly buttered 4-qt (4-l) baking dish, cover tightly with aluminum foil, and bake for 30 minutes. Uncover and continue to bake until the stuffing is hot throughout and lightly browned and crisp on top, 20–30 minutes longer. Serve hot.

To stuff or not to stuff

Roasting a bird unstuffed, with the stuffing baked separately, saves time and results in a more evenly cooked bird. If you decide to stuff your turkey, assemble the stuffing just before roasting so it can be put into the bird and then directly into the oven. Increase the roasting time of the turkey by 35–40 minutes, and make sure that the stuffing reaches an internal temperature of 165°F (74°C) on an instant-read thermometer. Place the remaining stuffing in a small buttered baking dish and bake as directed.

1 loaf sourdough bread, 1 lb (500 g), cut into ½-inch (12-mm) cubes with crust intact (about 10 cups)

¾ cup (6 oz/185 g) unsalted butter

2 large yellow onions, about 1 lb (500 g) total weight, finely chopped

1½ cups (9 oz/280 g) finely chopped celery, including some leafy tops

2 large Granny Smith apples, about 1 lb (500 g) total weight, halved, cored, and diced

2 tablespoons chopped fresh sage

1 teaspoon dried thyme

½ teaspoon freshly grated nutmeg

Salt

½ teaspoon freshly ground pepper

⅓ cup (½ oz/15 g) minced fresh flat-leaf (Italian) parsley

3 large eggs, lightly beaten

2½ cups (20 fl oz/625 ml) chicken stock or reduced-sodium chicken broth

SERVES 8–10

WILD RICE AND LEEK PILAF

This flavorful pilaf can be prepared on the stove top or baked in the oven. If you like, add ½ cup (3 oz/90 g) golden raisins or dried cranberries to the wild rice at the beginning of cooking and finish the dish with a sprinkling of toasted slivered almonds.

In a large saucepan over medium heat, warm the olive oil. Add the leek and onion and sauté until soft, 8–10 minutes. Add the wild rice, thyme, and salt and season to taste with pepper. Pour in the stock, bring to a boil, reduce the heat to medium-low, cover, and cook until the wild rice is tender, about 50 minutes.

Transfer to a warmed serving bowl. Serve hot.

A side or a stuffing

Rich and nutty, this pilaf is a classic accompaniment to roast chicken, turkey, or pork. It is especially delicious served in the hollowed-out shells of tomatoes or bell peppers (capsicums). Simply cut off the top third of a tomato or pepper and use a spoon to remove the insides. Fill each shell with the cooked pilaf, cover loosely with aluminum foil, and bake at 350°F (180°C) until tender, about 25 minutes for tomatoes or 45 minutes for peppers.

3 tablespoons olive oil or unsalted butter

1 large leek, white and tender green parts, halved lengthwise and thinly sliced crosswise

½ cup (2½ oz/75 g) finely chopped yellow onion

2 cups (12 oz/375 g) wild rice

1 teaspoon dried thyme

¾ teaspoon salt

Freshly ground pepper

6 cups (48 fl oz/1.5 l) chicken or turkey stock or reduced-sodium chicken broth

SERVES 8–10

COLLARD GREENS PIQUANT

This is a classic side dish in the American South, where collard greens are widely grown. The slightly bitter greens are simmered until tender and given a splash of vinegar for an extra lift. Wash the greens thoroughly to remove any sand.

In a large pot over medium heat, warm 1 tablespoon of the olive oil. Add the onion and sauté until soft, about 5 minutes. Add the greens and 2 cups (16 fl oz/500 ml) water. Cover and simmer until tender, about 20 minutes. Drain thoroughly and return the pot of greens to medium heat. Season to taste with salt and pepper. Drizzle with the vinegar and the remaining 3 tablespoons olive oil and heat through, tossing to mix. Serve warm.

A robust side

Serve these greens alongside spiced or herbed dishes that can stand up to their assertive flavor. They are also a nice accompaniment to fried or grilled fish, such as the Grilled Halibut with Potato-Fennel Purée (page 184).

4 tablespoons (2 fl oz/60 ml) extra-virgin olive oil

1 yellow onion, chopped

About 4 lb (2 kg) collard and mustard greens, tough stems removed

Salt and freshly ground pepper

¼ cup (2 fl oz/60 ml) balsamic vinegar

SERVES 8–10

BROCCOLI AND BLUE CHEESE GRATIN

Choose a mild blue cheese, such as Bleu d'Auvergne or Gorgonzola, for this recipe. The broccoli is first steamed until tender, then cloaked with cheese sauce and topped with buttery crumbs for baking. You can steam the broccoli and prepare the sauce in advance, then finish and bake the dish just before serving.

Preheat the oven to 350°F (180°C). Lightly butter a large gratin or baking dish.

Trim and discard the thick stalks from the broccoli. Cut the heads in half lengthwise. Place the broccoli in a steamer rack set over boiling water. Cover and steam until easily pierced with a fork, about 15 minutes. Drain and rinse under cold running water, then coarsely chop. Drain again, transfer to a bowl, and set aside.

In a frying pan over medium heat, melt 1 tablespoon of the butter. Add the bread crumbs and cook, stirring, until golden brown, about 5 minutes. Remove from the heat and set aside.

In a saucepan over medium-high heat, melt 4½ tablespoons (2¼ oz/67 g) of the butter. When the butter has melted, remove the pan from the heat and whisk in the flour until smooth. Return the pan to low heat and slowly pour in 1 cup (8 fl oz/250 ml) of the milk, whisking constantly. Reduce the heat to low and simmer, stirring occasionally, until thickened, 7–10 minutes. Whisk in another 1 cup milk. Add the salt, black pepper, and cayenne pepper. Continue to simmer, stirring occasionally, until the mixture has thickened again, 5–7 minutes. Whisk in the remaining 1 cup milk and simmer until thick enough to coat the back of a spoon, about 5 minutes longer. Stir in the blue cheese and cook, stirring, just until melted, about 2 minutes. Remove from the heat.

Pour the sauce over the broccoli and turn gently to mix. Spoon the mixture into the prepared gratin dish, smooth the surface, and top with the buttered bread crumbs. Cut the remaining 1 tablespoon butter into bits and dot the top. Bake until bubbling around the edges and golden on top, about 20 minutes. Serve hot.

6 heads broccoli, about 4 lb (2 kg) total weight

6½ tablespoons (3¼ oz/ 97 g) unsalted butter

¾ cup (1½ oz/45 g) fresh bread crumbs

4½ tablespoons (1½ oz/ 45 g) all-purpose (plain) flour

3 cups (24 fl oz/750 ml) whole milk

1 teaspoon fine sea salt

1 teaspoon freshly ground black pepper

⅛ teaspoon cayenne pepper

3 oz (90 g) blue cheese, crumbled

SERVES 12–14

BRUSSELS SPROUTS WITH PANCETTA AND ONIONS

Pairing roasted Brussels sprouts with caramelized onions brings out the sprouts' natural sweetness, as does the balsamic vinegar. The tangy saltiness of the pancetta balances the flavors. Be sure not to overcook the Brussels sprouts or they will become mushy and fade to a dull green.

Cut the onions crosswise into very thin slices, using a mandoline if possible, then cut the slices in half and set aside. In a frying pan over medium-high heat, cook the pancetta, stirring occasionally, until it is crisp and has released its fat, 8–10 minutes. Using a slotted spoon, transfer the cooked pancetta to a small plate lined with paper towels to drain and set aside.

Preheat the oven to 450°F (230°C). Add the butter and 1 tablespoon of the olive oil to the fat in the pan. Add the onions, reduce the heat to low, and cook uncovered, stirring occasionally, until deep golden brown, about 20 minutes. Remove from the heat and set aside. (The onions can be cooked up to 1 day in advance, covered, and refrigerated. When ready to use, reheat with 1 teaspoon olive oil.)

Meanwhile, put the Brussels sprouts in a bowl and add the remaining 1½ tablespoons olive oil and 1 teaspoon of the balsamic vinegar. Stir well to coat. Sprinkle with the salt and pepper. Transfer the Brussels sprouts to a nonstick baking sheet and spread in a single layer. Roast until tender when pierced with a fork and the edges are lightly browned, about 20 minutes.

Add the roasted Brussels sprouts to the onions along with the reserved pancetta and remaining 1 teaspoon balsamic vinegar. Cook over medium heat, turning to mix well, until the flavors are blended, 4–5 minutes. Transfer to a warmed serving dish and serve at once.

½ lb (250 g) yellow onions

½ lb (250 g) thinly sliced pancetta, cut into ½-inch (12-mm) pieces

2 tablespoons unsalted butter

2½ tablespoons extra-virgin olive oil

2 lb (1 kg) Brussels sprouts, halved lengthwise

2 teaspoons balsamic vinegar

½ teaspoon salt

½ teaspoon freshly ground pepper

SERVES 6–8

APPLE-PEAR CRISP

Preheat the oven to 375°F (190°C). Butter
a 9-by-13-inch (23-by-33-cm) baking dish.

Halve and core each apple, then cut into 1-inch
(2.5-cm) cubes. Repeat with the pears. Put all the
fruit in the prepared dish. Drizzle with the lemon
juice, turning the fruit once or twice to mix well.
Spread the fruit evenly in the dish.

In a bowl, stir together the flour, brown sugar, and
salt. Add the butter and, using a pastry blender
or 2 knives, cut the butter into the dry ingredients
until the mixture is grainy and the butter pieces
are about the size of small peas. Add the pine nuts
and mix with a fork or your fingers. Spread the
topping evenly over the fruit.

Bake until bubbling around the edges and golden
on top, about 50 minutes. Remove from the oven
and let cool on a wire rack for 10–15 minutes.
Serve warm with a dollop of whipped cream.

1 lb (500 g) apples, peeled

1 lb (500 g) pears, peeled

2 teaspoons fresh
lemon juice

3/4 cup (4 oz/125 g)
all-purpose (plain) flour

2/3 cup (5 oz/155 g) firmly
packed light brown sugar

1/8 teaspoon salt

1/4 cup (2 oz/60 g) chilled
unsalted butter, cut into
1/2-inch (12-mm) cubes

2 tablespoons pine nuts

Lightly whipped cream
for serving

SERVES 6–8

APPLE AND CRANBERRY GALETTE

This beautiful open-faced pastry glistens with scarlet cranberries nestled among golden apple slices. Cranberries and apples, both abundant during the cooler months, are the quintessential autumn pairing. Filled with already-simmered fruit, the galettes bake quickly and evenly.

To make the pastry, combine the flour, cornmeal, sugar, and salt in a food processor. Scatter the chunks of butter over the top and pulse for a few seconds until the butter pieces are the size of small peas. In a small bowl, whisk together the sour cream and ice water. Drizzle the mixture over the dough and pulse for a few seconds until the dough is smooth and clings together. Pat the dough into a ball, wrap in plastic wrap, and refrigerate for 20 minutes.

Meanwhile, to make the fruit filling, peel, core, and slice the apples. In a large frying pan over medium heat, combine ½ cup (4 fl oz/125 ml) water with the sugar, honey, lemon juice, and cinnamon and heat, stirring, until the sugar dissolves. Stir in the apple slices and simmer until opaque, 5–7 minutes. Using a slotted spoon, transfer the apple slices to a bowl and let cool slightly. Add the cranberries to the juices in the frying pan and simmer until they start to pop, about 2 minutes. Transfer the cranberries to the bowl of apples. Boil the juices over medium-high heat until reduced slightly and spoon over the fruit.

Position 2 racks in the middle of the oven and preheat to 400°F (200°C). Have ready 2 ungreased baking sheets or pizza pans.

Divide the ball of chilled pastry dough in half. On a lightly floured work surface, roll out each half into a round about 12 inches (30 cm) in diameter. Fold each pastry round in half, transfer to the baking sheets, and unfold. Divide the fruit filling equally between the pastry rounds and spread it in an even layer, leaving a 1½-inch (4-cm) border uncovered. Fold the border over the fruit, pleating the edges to form a broad rim. Lay thin slices of butter over the exposed fruit.

Bake the galettes, switching the pans between the racks and rotating them 180 degrees at the midway point, until the pastry is golden brown and the apples are tender, 35–40 minutes. Let cool completely on the pans on wire racks. Cover and store at room temperature until serving. Sprinkle with sugar, if desired.

Pastry

1¾ cups (9 oz/280 g) all-purpose (plain) flour

6 tablespoons (2 oz/60 g) white cornmeal

2 teaspoons sugar

¾ teaspoon salt

¾ cup (6 oz/185 g) cold unsalted butter, cut into chunks

6 tablespoons (3 oz/90 g) sour cream

½ cup (4 fl oz/125 ml) ice water

Filling

8 large Granny Smith apples, about 4 lb (2 kg) total weight

½ cup (4 oz/125 g) sugar

3 tablespoons honey

3 tablespoons fresh lemon juice

½ teaspoon ground cinnamon

1½ cups (6 oz/185 g) fresh cranberries

2 tablespoons unsalted butter, cut into thin slices

Sugar for dusting (optional)

MAKES TWO 9-INCH (23-CM) GALETTES; SERVES 10–12

PEAR TART TATIN WITH BRANDIED CREAM

For this decorative open-face tart, select firm but ripe Anjou or Bosc pears for the best baking. The original version of this tart, from France, was made with apples, but pears are a lovely substitute. Pear brandy heightens the flavor of the fruit and laces the whipped cream topping.

To make the pastry, in a food processor, combine the flour, granulated sugar, salt, butter, and shortening. Pulse until the butter pieces are the size of peas. Sprinkle with the ice water and pulse 3 or 4 times to incorporate. Transfer to a lightly floured surface and knead into a ball. Wrap in plastic wrap and refrigerate for 30 minutes.

Preheat the oven to 400°F (200°C). Peel, halve, and core the pears lengthwise and cut each half in half again; you should have 12 pieces of pear. Place in a bowl, add the pear brandy, and toss gently. Set aside.

On a lightly floured work surface, roll out the dough into a round 10 inches (25 cm) in diameter. Drape the pastry round over the rolling pin, transfer to a baking sheet, and refrigerate for 20 minutes.

In a 10-inch (25-cm) ovenproof frying pan over medium-high heat, melt the butter. Stir in the granulated sugar and corn syrup and cook, stirring occasionally and shaking the pan, until the syrup turns a golden amber, about 7 minutes. Remove from the heat and arrange the pear quarters, cut side down, in the pan in a pinwheel design. Sprinkle lightly with nutmeg. Lay the chilled pastry round over the top and cut 3 slits to let the steam escape. Tuck the edges of the pastry down slightly between the pears and the pan rim to make a pretty edge.

Bake until the pastry is golden brown and the pears are tender (test with a knife tip through a slit in the top), about 30 minutes. Remove from the oven and let cool for 1 minute. Invert a large serving plate on top of the pan. Holding the pan and the plate firmly, quickly invert them together. Lift off the pan, revealing the pears on top. Spoon any extra caramel from the pan over the pears.

To make the brandied cream, using an electric mixer on medium-high speed, beat the cream until soft peaks form. Fold in the confectioners' sugar and brandy. Serve the tart warm or at room temperature with the whipped cream.

Pastry

1¼ cups (6½ oz/200 g) all-purpose (plain) flour

1 tablespoon granulated sugar

⅛ teaspoon salt

5 tablespoons (2½ oz/75 g) cold unsalted butter, cut into ½-inch (12-mm) pieces

2 tablespoons cold solid vegetable shortening

3 tablespoons ice water

Filling

3 large, firm but ripe Anjou or Bosc pears, about 2 lb (1 kg) total weight

2½ tablespoons pear brandy or Cognac

2 tablespoons unsalted butter

½ cup (4 oz/125 g) granulated sugar

1 teaspoon light corn syrup

Freshly grated nutmeg

Brandied Cream

½ cup (4 fl oz/125 ml) heavy (double) cream

2 tablespoons confectioners' (icing) sugar, sifted

2 tablespoons pear brandy or Cognac

SERVES 8–10

PECAN PRALINE PIE

A caramelized topping of pecan praline embellishes this classic Southern favorite. Don't be intimidated by the crust; this pastry is easy to handle. You can make the pastry and line the pie dish up to a day ahead. Wrap the lined dish tightly in plastic wrap and refrigerate until ready to bake.

Preheat the oven to 400°F (200°C).

To make the pastry, in a food processor, combine the flour, granulated sugar, and butter and process until the mixture resembles fine crumbs. Add the egg yolk and pulse until blended. Add the ice water and pulse just until the dough forms a ball.

On a lightly floured work surface, roll out the dough into a round 12 inches (30 cm) in diameter. Drape the round over the rolling pin, transfer it to a 9-inch (23-cm) pie dish, and ease it into the bottom and up the sides. Trim the edges, leaving a 1-inch (2.5-cm) overhang. Fold the overhang under itself and flute the edges. Refrigerate the shell until firm, about 30 minutes or up to overnight. Line it with aluminum foil and fill with pie weights or dried beans. Bake for 15–20 minutes; the shell should be dry and still pale. Remove the weights and foil. Let the shell cool on a wire rack. Reduce the oven temperature to 350°F (180°C).

To make the filling, in a large bowl, beat the eggs with a whisk. Add the corn syrup, brown sugar, molasses, melted butter, Cognac, and salt and whisk until smooth. Scatter the chopped pecans evenly in the cooled pastry shell. Pour the egg mixture over the nuts. Bake until the top is browned, the filling is almost set, and a knife inserted into the center comes out almost clean, 45–50 minutes. Let cool on a wire rack.

To make the topping, in a small saucepan over medium heat, melt the butter. Add the pecans, sprinkle with the granulated sugar, and heat, stirring, until the nuts are toasted and caramelized, about 15 minutes. Pour onto a plate, spread into a single layer, and let cool. Scatter over the top of the pie. To serve, cut the pie into wedges and top with a dollop of whipped cream.

Pastry

1¼ cups (6½ oz/200 g) all-purpose (plain) flour

1 tablespoon granulated sugar

½ cup (4 oz/125 g) cold unsalted butter, cut into small pieces

1 large egg yolk

1½ tablespoons ice water

Filling

3 large eggs

¾ cup (7½ fl oz/235 ml) dark corn syrup

⅔ cup (5 oz/155 g) firmly packed light brown sugar

¼ cup (3 oz/90 g) unsulfured light molasses

¼ cup (2 oz/60 g) unsalted butter, melted and cooled

1 tablespoon Cognac

¼ teaspoon salt

1¾ cups (7 oz/220 g) coarsely chopped pecans

Praline Pecan Topping

2 tablespoons unsalted butter

1½ cups (6 oz/185 g) coarsely chopped pecans

¼ cup (2 oz/60 g) granulated sugar

Whipped cream for serving

SERVES 8–10

PUMPKIN CHEESECAKE

A gingersnap crust underlies this spicy cheesecake, and caramel-coated pecans adorn the top, for an irresistible alternative to traditional pumpkin pie. Cut this rich dessert into small wedges to serve. Perfect for an autumnal dinner party, the cheesecake can be made a day in advance, covered, and stored in the refrigerator until ready to serve.

Preheat the oven to 350°F (180°C). Lightly butter a 9-inch (23-cm) springform pan.

To make the crust, in a food processor, combine the gingersnaps and pecans and process until crumbly. Add the brown sugar and melted butter and pulse for a few seconds to blend. Transfer the crumb mixture to the prepared springform pan. Use your fingers to pat the mixture evenly over the bottom and up the sides of the pan. Refrigerate for 20 minutes.

To make the filling, in a small bowl, stir together the brown sugar, cinnamon, allspice, ginger, and cloves. In a large bowl, beat the cream cheese with an electric mixer on medium speed until smooth and creamy. Using a rubber spatula, occasionally scrape down the sides of the bowl. Gradually add the brown sugar mixture, beating until smooth. Beat in the eggs one at a time, beating well after each addition. Add the pumpkin purée, beating until smooth. Using the rubber spatula, scrape the batter into the chilled crust and smooth the top.

Bake the cheesecake until set or until a knife inserted into the center comes out clean, 35–40 minutes. Let cool completely on a wire rack. Cover and refrigerate until ready to serve.

To make the topping, set aside 10 pecan halves and coarsely chop the rest. In a small frying pan over medium-high heat, melt the butter. Add all of the pecans, sprinkle with the granulated sugar, and cook, stirring, until the sugar melts and the nuts are toasted and caramel coated. Transfer the nut mixture to a plate and let cool completely. Store in an airtight container. Just before serving, sprinkle the chopped pecans over the cheesecake and arrange the halves evenly around the perimeter.

Gingersnap Crust

¼ lb (125 g) gingersnaps, about 20 small cookies

⅓ cup (1½ oz/45 g) pecan halves

¼ cup (2 oz/60 g) firmly packed light brown sugar

¼ cup (2 oz/60 g) unsalted butter, melted

Filling

¾ cup (6 oz/185 g) firmly packed light brown sugar

1 teaspoon ground cinnamon

¼ teaspoon ground allspice

¼ teaspoon ground ginger

¼ teaspoon ground cloves

1 lb (500 g) cream cheese, at room temperature

3 large eggs

1 cup (8 oz/250 g) pumpkin purée

Topping

½ cup (2 oz/60 g) pecan halves

1 tablespoon unsalted butter

2 tablespoons granulated sugar

SERVES 10–12

CHOCOLATE-HAZELNUT BROWNIES WITH ICE CREAM

The key to rich brownies is the quantity of cacao in the chocolate. Choose a chocolate with 62 to 75 percent cacao for the best results. You can substitute toasted walnuts for the hazelnuts. For brownie sundaes, top each brownie with a scoop of ice cream and drizzle with chocolate sauce.

Preheat the oven to 350°F (180°C). Butter an 8-inch (20-cm) square baking pan.

Spread the hazelnuts in a single layer on a baking sheet. Place in the oven and toast, stirring once or twice, until the skins start to darken and wrinkle, 12–15 minutes. Remove from the oven. When the nuts are cool enough to handle, wrap in a kitchen towel and rub vigorously to remove the skins. Some specks of skin will remain. Chop the nuts and set aside. (The hazelnuts can be toasted up to 2 days in advance and stored in an airtight container.)

Place the chocolate in a metal bowl set over, but not touching, barely simmering water in a saucepan. Heat, stirring occasionally, until the chocolate has melted and is smooth, about 2 minutes. Set the bowl aside.

In a large bowl, using an electric mixer on medium speed, beat the butter until fluffy, about 1 minute. Add the sugar and beat until well blended, about 1 minute. Add the eggs and vanilla and beat until well blended, about 1 minute longer. Add ¼ cup (1½ oz/45 g) of the flour and the salt and beat well. Add the remaining flour, ¼ cup at a time, beating well after each addition. Add the chocolate and beat until well blended and creamy. Stir in the hazelnuts.

Pour the batter into the prepared pan, spreading it evenly. Bake until puffed and a toothpick inserted in the middle comes out clean, 20–25 minutes. Remove from the oven and let cool in the pan on a wire rack.

To serve, cut into 2-inch (5-cm) squares. Place 2 squares on each dessert plate and add a scoop of ice cream.

¾ cup (4 oz/125 g) hazelnuts (filberts)

4 oz (125 g) good-quality semisweet (plain) chocolate

½ cup (4 oz/125 g) unsalted butter, at room temperature

1 cup (8 oz/250 g) sugar

2 large eggs, beaten

1 teaspoon vanilla extract

¾ cup (4 oz/125 g) all-purpose (plain) flour

⅛ teaspoon salt

1 pt (16 fl oz/500 ml) vanilla ice cream

SERVES 8

winter

drinks and starters

POMEGRANATE SPARKLERS 229

WINTER CITRUS SPRITZERS 229

ICED VIN DE CITRON 230

LEMON VODKA MARTINIS 230

VODKA METROPOLITANS 233

CLASSIC MARTINIS 233

CHAMPAGNE WITH LIQUEUR 234

CAMPARI AND SODA 234

EGGNOGG WITH NUTMEG AND CINNAMON 237

HOT SPICED RED WINE 237

OYSTERS ON THE HALF SHELL 240

GOLDEN BEETS WITH SMOKED TROUT AND DILL 243

BRIOCHE ROUNDS WITH CAVIAR 243

SHRIMP COCKTAILS 244

CUCUMBER WITH FRESH CRAB 244

PECORINO GOUGÈRES WITH PROSCIUTTO 247

GOAT CHEESE AND SHALLOT TOASTS 248

ROSEMARY ROASTED ALMONDS 248

ROASTED LAMB CHOPS WITH ROSEMARY
AND SEA SALT 251

CHICKEN LIVER MOUSSE WITH CORNICHONS 252

soups and salads

GOLDEN BEET SOUP WITH CRÈME FRAÎCHE 255

SHRIMP BISQUE 256

ORANGE, AVOCADO, AND FENNEL SALAD 259

ARUGULA, RADICCHIO, AND ESCAROLE SALAD 259

CRAB SALAD WITH APPLES AND GRAPEFRUIT COULIS 260

FRISÉE, ENDIVE, AND WATERCRESS SALAD
WITH ROQUEFORT 263

mains and sides

SHRIMP, SCALLOPS, AND STUFFED SQUID 264

BAKED GNOCCHI WITH TALEGGIO, PANCETTA,
AND SAGE 267

BAKED HAM WITH HONEY-PORT GLAZE 268

BOURBON-GLAZED HAM 268

STANDING RIB ROAST WITH GARLIC-PEPPERCORN CRUST 271

BRAISED SHORT RIBS 272

BEEF TENDERLOIN WITH SHALLOT AND
SYRAH REDUCTION 275

HERBED YORKSHIRE PUDDING 276

BRAISED BRUSSELS SPROUTS WITH SAGE 276

POLENTA WITH WHITE CHEDDAR 279

SWISS CHARD GRATIN 279

CREAMY GRATIN OF WINTER VEGETABLES 280

ROASTED CAULIFLOWER WITH GREEN OLIVES 283

ROASTED POTATOES WITH SEA SALT 283

desserts

CHOCOLATE FRANGELICO TRUFFLES 284

APPLE-GINGER TART WITH CIDER-BOURBON SAUCE 287

STEAMED FIG PUDDING 288

WINTER COMPOTE WITH CLOVE BISCOTTI 291

RICOTTA CHEESECAKE WITH BLOOD ORANGE GLAZE 292

GINGERBREAD WITH WHIPPED CREAM 295

POMEGRANATE SPARKLERS

Chill 4 martini glasses. Fill a tall cocktail shaker half full with ice. Add ¼ cup (2 fl oz/60 ml) each of the pomegranate syrup and lime juice. Cover and shake for 20 seconds. Strain into a glass and top with sparkling water. Repeat to fill 3 more glasses. Garnish each glass with a lime slice and a sprinkling of pomegranate seeds. Serve at once.

Ice cubes

1 cup (8 fl oz/250 ml) pomegranate syrup

1 cup (8 fl oz/250 ml) fresh lime juice (8–10 limes)

1 bottle (24 fl oz/750 ml) sparkling water, chilled

Thin lime slices for garnish

Pomegranate seeds for garnish

SERVES 4

WINTER CITRUS SPRITZERS

In a large pitcher, combine the grapefruit and orange juices. Add 2 or 3 ice cubes to each of 6 tall glasses. Stir the lime juice into the juice mixture and divide evenly among the glasses. Fill the glasses with the sparkling mineral water and garnish with citrus slices. Let guests add sugar to taste to their glasses.

2 cups (16 fl oz/500 ml) fresh grapefruit juice

2 cups (16 fl oz/500 ml) fresh orange juice

12–18 ice cubes

¼ cup (2 fl oz/60 ml) fresh lime juice

4 cups (32 fl oz/1 l) sparkling water, chilled

Citrus slices for garnish, quartered

Superfine (caster) sugar

SERVES 6

ICED VIN DE CITRON

In this refreshing nonalcoholic cocktail, lemon cuts the sweetness of grape juice, and mint provides a touch of color and hit of fresh flavor. The recipe can be doubled and made ahead in a pitcher, and then poured over ice to serve.

If making lemon zest ice cubes, use a bar-style lemon stripper to remove a strip of peel about 4 inches (10 cm) long from 1 of the lemons. Repeat until there is no more peel on the lemon, then repeat with 6 or 7 more lemons until you have 24 strips. Tie each strip of peel in a loose single knot to create 24 knots. Place a knot in each compartment of two 12-well ice-cube trays, fill with water, and freeze until solid.

Chill 8 glasses in the freezer for 15 minutes.

Pour ½ cup (4 fl oz/125 ml) grape juice into each chilled glass, add 1½ tablespoons lemon juice, and 3 ice cubes. Garnish each glass with a mint sprig.

Fruitful ice

Decorative ice cubes add both color and flavor to any drink. Choose from citrus wedges or zest, melon balls, berries, or fresh herbs. Place the item in ice cube trays, fill with water, and freeze. Filtered or bottled water will give you the clearest cubes.

7 or 8 lemons for lemon zest ice cubes (optional)

4 cups (32 fl oz/1 l) white grape juice, chilled

¾ cup (6 fl oz/180 ml) fresh lemon juice

8 fresh mint sprigs for garnish

SERVES 8

LEMON VODKA MARTINIS

The use of lemon vodka makes it a snap to prepare this cocktail, but unflavored vodka could be used instead—simply rub the glass with a lemon wedge before adding the liquor. Caper berries make an interesting and flavorful garnish.

Chill 8 small martini glasses in the freezer for 15 minutes.

For each serving, put several ice cubes in a cocktail shaker and add ¼ cup (2 fl oz/60 ml) of the vodka and 1 teaspoon or less of the vermouth. Shake vigorously and strain into a chilled martini glass. Garnish with a caper berry.

Infusing vodkas

You can infuse vodka with a wide range of fresh ingredients, from berries to herbs to peppers. The general process involves allowing the infuser to mingle with the vodka in an airtight container for about a week. To make a lemon-infused vodka, start with 2–3 lemons; wash, slice (to release their flavor), and remove any seeds. Place them in an airtight glass container, fill with vodka, seal, and store in a cool dark place for 5–7 days.

Ice cubes

2 cups (16 fl oz/500 ml) lemon vodka, chilled

8 teaspoons dry vermouth, or to taste

8 caper berries, with stems intact, for garnish

SERVES 8

VODKA METROPOLITANS

Chill 4 martini glasses. Fill a tall cocktail shaker half full with ice. Pour in half each of the vodka, lime juice, and cranberry juice. Cover with the lid and shake for 20 seconds. Strain into 2 of the chilled glasses and garnish each with a lime wedge. Repeat to make 2 more drinks. Serve at once.

Ice cubes

1¼ cups (10 fl oz/310 ml) black currant–flavored vodka

½ cup (4 fl oz/125 ml) fresh lime juice

¼ cup (2 fl oz/60 ml) cranberry juice

4 lime wedges for garnish

SERVES 4

CLASSIC MARTINIS

Chill 4 martini glasses. Fill a tall cocktail shaker half full with ice. Pour in half each of the gin and vermouth. Cover with the lid and shake for 20 seconds. Strain into 2 of the chilled glasses and garnish each with an olive or two on a cocktail pick. Repeat to make 2 more drinks. Serve at once.

Ice cubes

1¾ cups (14 fl oz/ 430 ml) gin

¼ cup (2 fl oz/60 ml) dry vermouth

4–8 green olives for garnish

SERVES 4

CHAMPAGNE WITH LIQUEUR

Select 4 Champagne flutes. Pour 1 tablespoon of the desired liqueur into each glass. Top with about ½ cup (4 fl oz/125 ml) of the Champagne. Stir and serve at once.

¼ cup (2 fl oz/60 ml) framboise, crème de cassis, or amaretto

1 bottle (24 fl oz/750 ml) Champagne or other sparkling wine, chilled

SERVES 4

CAMPARI AND SODA

Chill 6 glasses in the freezer for 15 minutes.

In each glass, place 2 or 3 ice cubes and pour in ¼ cup (2 fl oz/60 ml) of the Campari. Add ⅓ cup (3 fl oz/80 ml) of the soda water, or more to taste, stir, and garnish with a citrus peel.

12–18 ice cubes

1½ cups (12 fl oz/ 375 ml) Campari

1 bottle (16 fl oz/ 500 ml) soda water, or as needed, chilled

Thin strips of orange or lemon peel for garnish

SERVES 6

EGGNOG WITH NUTMEG AND CINNAMON

A quintessential holiday drink, eggnog evokes images of festive gatherings during the winter. Here, the warming cocktail is topped with sweetened whipped cream and freshly ground spices.

Using a nutmeg grater or the smallest rasps on a handheld grater-shredder, grate the nutmeg until you have about 1 teaspoon powder. In a spice grinder or a coffee grinder reserved for spices, grind the cinnamon stick. Set aside.

In a large saucepan, whisk together the egg yolks, 2 cups (16 fl oz/500 ml) of the milk, and 1 cup (8 oz/250 g) of the sugar. Place over low heat and simmer, stirring often, until slightly thickened, 8–10 minutes. Remove from the heat, stir in the remaining 2 cups milk, and let cool.

In a bowl, using a handheld mixer or whisk, whip the cream with the remaining ¼ cup (2 oz/60 g) sugar and the vanilla until soft peaks form. Set aside.

Strain the cooled mixture through a fine-mesh sieve and pour into a serving pitcher or a small punch bowl. Stir in the brandy. Serve the eggnog in cups or glasses, topped with a dollop of the whipped cream and a sprinkle each of nutmeg and cinnamon.

1 or 2 whole nutmegs

1 cinnamon stick

12 large egg yolks

4 cups (32 fl oz/1 l) whole milk

1¼ cups (10 oz/310 g) sugar

2 cups (16 fl oz/500 ml) heavy (double) cream

½ teaspoon vanilla extract

1½ cups (12 fl oz/375 ml) brandy, Cognac, rum, or bourbon

SERVES 8–10

HOT SPICED RED WINE

Flavored with whole spices and citrus and sweetened with sugar, hot spiced red wine makes a welcoming holiday drink for guests. This recipe features cinnamon, cloves, star anise, and vanilla, as well as thick slices of fragrant orange zest.

Remove the zest from the oranges in strips about ½ inch (12 mm) wide. Set aside 2 long strips. Cut the remaining strips into 12–14 pieces each 1½–2 inches (4–5 cm) long, then cut a small slit in each so that the zest can be slipped onto the rim of a glass as a garnish.

In a nonreactive saucepan, combine the wine, the 2 long orange zest strips, the cinnamon sticks, cloves, star anise, vanilla bean pieces,

and sugar. Place over medium-high heat and bring almost to a boil, stirring to dissolve the sugar. Reduce the heat to low and simmer for 5 minutes to blend the flavors.

Serve from the stove or pour the mixture into a small punch bowl and ladle servings into heat-resistant glasses. Slip a piece of zest on the rim of each glass.

2 oranges

2 bottles (48 fl oz/1.5 l) Syrah or Merlot

2 cinnamon sticks, about 4 inches (10 cm) long

8 whole cloves

2 whole star anise

2 pieces vanilla bean, about 2 inches (5 cm) long

½ cup (4 oz/125 g) sugar

SERVES 12–14

OYSTERS ON THE HALF SHELL

To make the mignonette sauce, in a small bowl, stir together the vinegar, lemon juice, shallot, and peppercorns. Season to taste with salt. Cover and refrigerate until serving. (The sauce can be prepared in advance, covered, and refrigerated for up to 24 hours.)

To serve, cover a large metal serving tray with crushed ice. Arrange the shucked oysters on the tray, nestling the shells in the ice. Transfer the sauce to a small serving bowl and nestle it in the ice on the tray with the oysters. Place a spoon into the sauce and serve at once.

Selecting oysters

For party fare, serve a variety of oysters, such as small, sweet Kumamotos, Malpeques, and a local variety. Place the opened oysters on a platter of crushed ice and offer small forks and the mignonette sauce alongside.

Mignonette

²/₃ cup (5 fl oz/160 ml) white wine vinegar

2 tablespoons fresh lemon juice

1 tablespoon finely chopped shallot

1 tablespoon drained brined green peppercorns, chopped

Sea salt

Crushed ice

18 oysters, shucked

SERVES 6

GOLDEN BEETS WITH SMOKED TROUT AND DILL

The beets can be cooked and sliced the day before—then all that is required the day of the party is quick assembly. Red beets can be used as well, but they will tint the edges of the cream cheese pink.

Preheat the oven to 350°F (180°C).

Put the beets in a shallow baking dish, drizzle with the olive oil, and sprinkle with the salt. Turn to coat well. Roast until the beets are easily pierced with a fork, about 80 minutes. Let cool.

Slip off the skins and slice the beets into rounds ¼ inch (6 mm) thick. Top each slice with about ½ teaspoon cream cheese, a piece of smoked trout, and a sprinkle of dill. If desired, put each assembled round atop a cracker. Arrange on a platter and serve.

12 golden beets, each 1½–2 inches (4–5 cm) in diameter

2 tablespoons extra-virgin olive oil

1 teaspoon sea salt

4 oz (125 g) cream cheese, at room temperature, or crème fraîche

1 smoked trout fillet, about 5 oz (155 g), broken into bite-sized pieces

¼ cup (⅓ oz/10 g) minced fresh dill

2 packages water crackers for serving (optional)

SERVES 14–16

BRIOCHE ROUNDS WITH CAVIAR

Very tender and light, brioche bread makes perfect toasts for delicate toppings. If you cannot find brioche, thin-sliced white sandwich bread is a good alternative. Use fancifully shaped cookie cutters if desired.

Preheat the oven to 400°F (200°C). Have ready an ungreased large baking sheet.

Using a 1½-inch (4-cm) round or shaped biscuit cutter, cut 4 rounds from each bread slice. Arrange the rounds on the baking sheet. Bake, turning once, until lightly golden on both sides, about 20 minutes. Set aside.

When ready to serve, spread each toast with about ½ teaspoon of the crème fraîche, top with a little caviar, and garnish with a light sprinkle of chives.

15 thin slices brioche or white sandwich bread

¾ cup (6 oz/185 g) crème fraîche

1½ oz (45 g) golden caviar or salmon roe

¼ cup (⅓ oz/10 g) cut-up fresh chives (1-inch/2.5-cm lengths)

SERVES 14–16

SHRIMP COCKTAILS

Seafood aficionados tend to love shrimp cocktail. In this version, the shrimp are served in individual cocktail glasses on a bed of shredded lettuce, making them easy to eat at a party. For a milder sauce, reduce the amount of chile sauce.

In a bowl, stir together the ketchup, chile sauce, lemon juice, Worcestershire sauce, and vinegar and mix well. Set the sauce aside.

Select 12 glasses, such as cocktail glasses or short water glasses. Shred the romaine and divide among the glasses, making a bed in each. Put 4 of the shrimp in each glass and top with about 2 tablespoons of the sauce. Stick a celery rib, base down, into each glass. Cut the lemon slices in half, then cut a slit into the halves and slip one onto each glass rim. Serve at once.

1⅓ cups (11 fl oz/345 ml) ketchup

3 tablespoons Thai chile sauce

2 tablespoons fresh lemon juice

2 teaspoons each Worcestershire sauce and red wine vinegar

12 romaine (cos) lettuce leaves

48 cooked and peeled shrimp (prawns) with tail segments intact (about 2 lb/1 kg)

12 pale inner celery ribs

6 thin lemon slices for garnish

SERVES 12

CUCUMBER WITH FRESH CRAB

Here, thin slices of cucumber replace the typical crackers, delivering a fresh flavor and crunchy texture that complement the sweet crab. Olive oil–packed canned tuna or cooked chicken would make a fine substitute for the crab.

Peel 5 of the cucumbers and cut into slices ¼ inch (6 mm) thick. You should have 48 slices. Peel, halve, seed, and mince the remaining cucumber. Set aside.

Pick over the crabmeat and remove any shell fragments. Set aside. In a bowl, combine the mayonnaise, olive oil, lemon juice, shallots, tarragon, salt, and cayenne and mix well.

Add the crabmeat and turn gently with a fork to mix, being careful not to break up the crabmeat. Put about 1½ teaspoons of the crab mixture on each cucumber slice and top with a little of the minced cucumber.

Arrange on a platter, cover, and refrigerate for up to 2 hours before serving.

6 cucumbers

1½ cups (9 oz/280 g) fresh-cooked crabmeat

3½ tablespoons mayonnaise

1 teaspoon extra-virgin olive oil

1½ teaspoons fresh lemon juice

4 teaspoons minced shallots

2 teaspoons minced fresh tarragon

¼ teaspoon each salt and cayenne pepper

SERVES 10–12

PECORINO GOUGÈRES WITH PROSCIUTTO

These savory puffs are made with *pâte à choux*, or puff pastry, and then sliced open and filled with delicate shavings of cheese and prosciutto. Flavorful and filling, they are a crowd-pleasing small sandwich to serve at holiday cocktail gatherings, open houses, or any occasions that call for substantial finger food.

Preheat the oven to 425°F (220°C). Line 2 baking sheets with parchment (baking) paper.

In a saucepan over medium-high heat, combine 1 cup (8 fl oz/250 ml) water, the butter, salt, white pepper, and cayenne. Bring to a boil, stirring, and continue to cook until the butter is melted, 2–3 minutes. Add the flour and mix vigorously with a wooden spoon until a thick paste forms and pulls away from the side of the pan, about 3 minutes. Remove from the heat and make a well in the center. Crack 1 egg into the well and, using the wooden spoon or an electric handheld mixer, beat it into the hot mixture. Repeat with 3 more eggs, beating them in one at a time. Add the 2 tablespoons of grated cheese along with the fourth egg.

Fit a pastry bag with a ¹⁄₂-inch (12-mm) round tip and spoon about half of the egg mixture into it. Pipe the mixture onto the prepared baking sheets into rounds 1–1¹⁄₂ inches (2.5–4 cm) in diameter and about ¹⁄₂ inch (12 mm) high, spacing them 2 inches (5 cm) apart. Repeat with the remaining half of the mixture. You should have 30 rounds in all. (Alternatively, use a teaspoon to shape the gougères. Dip the spoon into a glass of cold water, then scoop up a generous teaspoon of the mixture and push it onto the baking sheet with your fingertips. Repeat, dipping the spoon in the water each time to prevent sticking.) In a small bowl, lightly beat the remaining egg. Brush the top of each gougère with a little of the beaten egg.

Bake for 10 minutes, then reduce the oven temperature to 350°F (180°C) and bake until the gougères are golden brown and crunchy, about 15 minutes longer. Do not underbake, or they will be mushy. When done, pierce each gougère with a wooden skewer, turn off the oven, and leave them in the oven for 10 minutes. Remove from the oven and let cool for at least 30 minutes on the baking sheets before filling.

Cut the prosciutto slices into 30 pieces. Using a vegetable peeler, shave the cheese into thin pieces. Cut each gougère in half and tuck in a folded piece of prosciutto and some shavings of cheese. They should look plump and well filled. Serve at once.

6 tablespoons (3 oz/90 g) unsalted butter

1 teaspoon salt

¹⁄₂ teaspoon ground white pepper

Pinch of cayenne pepper

1 cup (5 oz/155 g) all-purpose (plain) flour

5 large eggs

2 tablespoons finely grated pecorino romano cheese, plus 4-oz (125-g) block for shaving

3 oz (90 g) very thinly sliced prosciutto

SERVES 14–16

GOAT CHEESE AND SHALLOT TOASTS

The addition of sweet cream to soft goat cheese tempers its tanginess while making it light and easy to spread. Pink peppercorns scattered across the top add color and complement the shallots.

Preheat the oven to 350°F (180°C). Have ready 2 ungreased baking sheets.

Cut the baguette on the diagonal into slices ¼ inch (6 mm) thick. Arrange the slices in a single layer on the baking sheets. Bake, turning once, until lightly golden on both sides, about 25 minutes. Set aside.

Put the goat cheese in a bowl and mash it with a fork. Add 1 tablespoon of the cream and mash it in. Continue to add the cream, 1 tablespoon at a time, until you have a soft, mild spread. Mix in the salt and the shallots to taste.

When ready to serve, spread each baguette toast with the cheese and shallot spread and top with several pink peppercorns.

1 baguette

5 oz (155 g) soft goat cheese, at room temperature

4–6 tablespoons (2–3 fl oz/60–90 ml) heavy (double) cream

½ teaspoon salt

2 or 3 small shallots, minced

3 tablespoons pink peppercorns, smashed

SERVES 12–14

ROSEMARY ROASTED ALMONDS

For a less pronounced rosemary flavor, omit the minced rosemary and use only the sprigs. If desired, more sea salt and a few small sprigs of fresh rosemary can be added just before serving the almonds.

Preheat the oven to 350°F (180°C). Have ready an ungreased baking sheet.

In a bowl, combine the almonds, olive oil, salt, pepper, minced rosemary, and rosemary sprigs. Turn to coat the almonds well. Mound the mixture on the baking sheet. Roast, turning a few times, until the almonds are beginning to lightly brown, 20–25 minutes. Transfer the almonds to paper towels and let cool. Discard the rosemary sprigs. Transfer the cooled almonds to an airtight container lined with waxed paper and store in a cool, dry place for up to 2 weeks.

2¼ cups (12 oz/375 g) whole unblanched almonds

3 tablespoons extra-virgin olive oil

1 tablespoon sea salt

1 teaspoon freshly ground pepper

3 tablespoons minced fresh rosemary

4 fresh rosemary sprigs, each 6 inches (15 cm) long

SERVES 12–14

ROASTED LAMB CHOPS WITH ROSEMARY AND SEA SALT

In this recipe, racks of lamb are roasted, then cut into individual chops. Serve the bite-sized chops as casual finger food or offer small plates, knives, and forks. For an elegant presentation, ask your butcher to french the ribs—trim off the fat between each chop to expose the tips of the bones.

Preheat the oven to 475°F (245°C). Place 2 roasting pans, each large enough to hold 2 racks of lamb, in the oven. (Alternatively, use 4 baking dishes each large enough to hold a single rack of lamb.)

Rub the lamb and bones with the garlic cloves. Rub all over with the salt and pepper.

In each of 2 large, nonstick frying pans over medium heat, warm 2 tablespoons of the olive oil. When the oil is hot, add 2 of the lamb racks, fat side down, to each pan and sear for 1–2 minutes. Using tongs to turn and hold the lamb, sear both ends, about 1 minute on each end. Finally, sear the bone side for 1–2 minutes.

Transfer the lamb to a platter or cutting board and sprinkle all over with the chopped rosemary.

Cover the exposed bones with aluminum foil to keep them from charring. Place the racks, bone side down, in the warmed roasting pans. Roast until an instant-read thermometer inserted into the thickest part of the meat (but not touching bone) registers 130°–140°F (54°–60°C) for medium-rare, 13–15 minutes; or 140°–150°F (60°–65°C) for medium, 15–20 minutes.

Transfer the lamb to a cutting board and tent loosely with aluminum foil. Let rest for 7–10 minutes.

To serve, cut the racks into chops and arrange the chops on a warmed platter. Garnish with the rosemary sprigs.

4 racks of lamb, each
1½–1¾ lb (750–875 g)
with 7 or 8 ribs, frenched
(see note)

4 cloves garlic,
lightly crushed

2 tablespoons
coarse sea salt

4 teaspoons freshly
ground pepper

4 tablespoons
(2 fl oz/60 ml) olive oil

2 tablespoons finely chopped
fresh rosemary, plus several
sprigs for garnish

SERVES 14–16

CHICKEN LIVER MOUSSE WITH CORNICHONS

Simple yet sophisticated, chicken liver mousse goes together quickly and can be made up to 2 days in advance of the party, covered, and refrigerated. Just a quick stir is all that it needs before serving. For a richer mousse, substitute duck livers for the chicken livers.

In a large frying pan over medium heat, melt 3 tablespoons of the butter. When it foams, add the chicken livers and pepper and cook, stirring occasionally, until the livers are firm but still rosy inside, about 10 minutes. Remove the pan from the heat and pour in the warmed brandy. Light a long match and carefully hold it just above the pan, igniting the fumes. Return the pan to medium-high heat. Stir the livers and shake the pan slowly until most of the alcohol has evaporated, about 1 minute. Transfer to a food processor.

In the same pan over medium-low heat, melt 3 tablespoons of the butter. When it foams, add the shallots, apple, and thyme and cook, stirring occasionally, until the apple pieces are soft, about 20 minutes. Transfer to the food processor and let cool. Process until smooth. Add the ½ cup (4 oz/125 g) butter and the cream and process until a smooth purée forms.

Spoon the mousse into a ramekin just large enough to hold it and smooth the surface. Cover the ramekin and refrigerate for several hours until the mousse is firm.

To serve, stir the mousse briefly and then spread a small amount on each cracker. Top each cracker with 2 cornichon slivers and serve.

6 tablespoons (3 oz/90 g) plus ½ cup (4 oz/125 g) unsalted butter, at room temperature

1 lb (500 g) chicken livers, membranes removed and any soft or discolored spots trimmed

¼ teaspoon freshly ground pepper

⅓ cup (3 fl oz/80 ml) brandy, warmed

⅓ cup (1½ oz/45 g) coarsely chopped shallots

1 tart apple such as Granny Smith, peeled, cored, and coarsely chopped

1 teaspoon fresh thyme leaves

6 tablespoons (3 fl oz/90 ml) heavy (double) cream

36 water crackers

8–10 cornichons, cut lengthwise into thin slivers

SERVES 6

GOLDEN BEET SOUP WITH CRÈME FRAÎCHE

This striking soup makes an impressive starter for any dinner party. Roasting the beets deepens the flavor of the finished dish, and the garnish of salmon roe and crème fraîche adds a wonderful salty creaminess. For a perfectly smooth soup, pass it through a fine-mesh sieve after puréeing.

Preheat the oven to 350°F (180°C). If the beet greens are attached, cut them off, leaving 1 inch (2.5 cm) of the stem intact (reserve the greens for another use). Place the beets in a baking dish and drizzle with the olive oil. Sprinkle with the salt and pepper and spread in a single layer. Roast until tender when pierced with a fork, about 1½ hours, or longer if the beets are large. Let cool, remove and discard the skins, and coarsely chop. (The beets can be roasted up to 4 hours in advance.)

In a large saucepan, combine the beets and chicken stock. Bring to a boil over high heat, reduce the heat to low, and simmer until the beets are heated through, 10–15 minutes.

Purée the soup with a stand or immersion blender until smooth, reheat if necessary, and taste and adjust the seasoning.

Ladle the soup into warmed bowls. Top with a dollop of crème fraîche and a spoonful of roe. Garnish with the dill sprigs and serve.

Dressing up soup

A well-selected garnish, both stylish and delicious, can turn any soup into a special dish. A drizzle or dollop of crème fraîche, yogurt, or sour cream makes an elegant topping, especially when paired with a sprig of rosemary, spray of sage leaves, or sprinkle of thyme. Croutons can add crunch and flavor. Baby root vegetables, such as beets, carrot, and fennel, thinly sliced and fried, can add color and texture.

2 lb (1 kg) golden beets

1 tablespoon extra-virgin olive oil

1 teaspoon salt

1 teaspoon freshly ground pepper

5 cups (40 fl oz/1.25 l) chicken stock or reduced-sodium chicken broth

½ cup (4 oz/125 g) crème fraîche

3 oz (90 g) salmon roe

Fresh dill sprigs for garnish

SERVES 6–8

SHRIMP BISQUE

Rich and velvety, this seafood soup makes a warming starter in winter. It also pairs well with a citrusy salad for a light dinner. The secret to the bisque's intensity is a simple stock made from the shrimp cooking water, then reduced with the sautéed shrimp shells until a concentrated and rich flavor is achieved.

In a large, heavy saucepan or Dutch oven, combine 6 cups (48 fl oz/1.5 l) water, the thyme, parsley, onion, carrot, peppercorns, and bay leaves. Bring to a boil over medium-high heat. Add the shrimp and cook just until they turn opaque, 1–2 minutes. Using a slotted spoon, transfer the shrimp to a colander and rinse them under cold running water. Reduce the heat to low so the stock simmers.

Cover and refrigerate 8 shrimp in the shell for garnish. Peel the remaining shrimp, reserving the heads and shells. Coarsely chop the shrimp, cover, and refrigerate.

In a frying pan over medium-high heat, warm the olive oil. When hot, add all the shrimp heads and shells and sauté for 5–8 minutes. Reduce the heat to medium and continue to sauté for 15 minutes. Add the contents of the pan to the simmering stock and cook until reduced to about 2 cups (16 fl oz/500 ml), about 45 minutes. Using the slotted spoon, remove the herbs, vegetables, and shells and heads and discard. Add the wine, raise the heat to high, and bring to a boil. Reduce the heat to low and simmer, uncovered, until reduced to about 3 cups (24 fl oz/750 ml), 30–40 minutes. Add the salt. (The soup can be made up to this point a day ahead, cooled, and refrigerated. Bring to a simmer over medium heat before continuing.)

Add the cream, raise the heat to medium-high, and heat, stirring, until small bubbles form along the edge of the pan. Reduce the heat to medium and simmer, stirring frequently, until the soup is reduced to about 4 cups (32 fl oz/1 l) and is thick and creamy, about 20 minutes. Taste and adjust the seasoning with salt. Strain the soup through a chinois, a fine-mesh sieve, or cheesecloth (muslin). Pour into a clean saucepan and heat over medium heat, stirring, until small bubbles form along the edge of the pan. Remove from the heat and cover.

In a saucepan over low heat, gently reheat the chopped and whole shrimp. To serve, divide the chopped shrimp equally among warmed soup bowls. Ladle ½ cup (4 fl oz/125 ml) of the soup into each bowl. Float a whole shrimp in the center of each bowl and sprinkle with freshly ground pepper. Serve at once.

5 fresh thyme sprigs

5 fresh flat-leaf (Italian) parsley sprigs

1 small yellow onion, quartered

1 small carrot, peeled and quartered

8 peppercorns

2 bay leaves

1½ lb (750 g) shrimp (prawns), preferably with heads intact

⅓ cup (3 fl oz/80 ml) extra-virgin olive oil

1 bottle (24 fl oz/750 ml) Sauvignon Blanc

1 teaspoon fine sea salt

4 cups (32 fl oz/1 l) heavy (double) cream

Freshly ground pepper

SERVES 8

ORANGE, AVOCADO, AND FENNEL SALAD

Cut off the stems and feathery leaves from each fennel bulb. Reserve a few leaves for garnish. Trim the base and discard the bulb's outer layer, if tough. Finely slice the bulb crosswise into thin pieces. Halve, pit, and peel the avocados, then cut lengthwise into slices 1/2 inch (12 mm) thick. Peel each orange and separate the sections, removing any white pith and seeds. Halve the sections.

In a salad bowl, mix together the orange zest, olive oil, orange juice, 1 tablespoon of the balsamic vinegar, the salt, and the pepper. Add the fennel, oranges, avocados, and olives and toss gently. Divide among chilled salad plates. Drizzle each salad with a little of the remaining balsamic vinegar, garnish with the reserved fennel leaves, and serve.

2 fennel bulbs

3 avocados

5 mandarin oranges

2 teaspoons grated orange zest

3 tablespoons olive oil

1 tablespoon fresh orange juice

2 tablespoons white balsamic vinegar

1/2 teaspoon each sea salt and freshly ground pepper

1/2 cup (2 1/2 oz/75 g) oil-cured black olives, pitted

SERVES 6–8

ARUGULA, RADICCHIO, AND ESCAROLE SALAD

In the bottom of a large salad bowl, using a fork, mix together the olive oil and vinegars. Mix in the sea salt.

Tear the radicchio and escarole into bite-sized pieces and add to the bowl. Add the arugula and parsley leaves but do not toss. Just before serving, gently toss to coat the greens with the vinaigrette. Serve at once.

Winter salads

Bright, slightly bitter salads are a good match for winter's roasted meats, soups, and stews. In addition to the greens used here, try endive and mustard greens, mix in some fresh herbs, and toss with a citrusy vinaigrette.

1/4 cup (2 fl oz/60 ml) olive oil

1 tablespoon red wine vinegar

2 teaspoons balsamic vinegar

1/2 teaspoon sea salt

1/2 head radicchio

1 head escarole

1 cup (1 oz/30 g) baby arugula (rocket) leaves

1/2 cup (1/2 oz/15 g) fresh flat-leaf (Italian) parsley leaves

SERVES 6

CRAB SALAD WITH APPLES AND GRAPEFRUIT COULIS

Many types of apples and all grapefruit are at the height of their flavor during the winter months. Here, the apples are cut into matchsticks with a mandoline, but a sharp knife could be used as well. The syruplike grapefruit coulis can be drizzled on top or in a border around the crab.

Using a sharp knife, cut a slice from the top and bottom of the grapefruit to reveal the flesh. Stand the grapefruit upright on a cutting board and thickly slice off the peel and white pith in strips, following the contour of the fruit. Holding the grapefruit in one hand, cut along either side of each segment to release it from the membrane, letting the segments drop into a bowl. Set 2 grapefruit segments aside. Coarsely chop the rest of the segments.

In a saucepan, combine the chopped grapefruit with ¼ cup (2 fl oz/60 ml) water. Bring to a boil over medium-high heat, reduce the heat to low, and simmer, stirring, until soft, about 5 minutes. Purée in the pan with an immersion blender or transfer the mixture to a stand blender to purée. Strain the purée through a fine-mesh sieve into a clean saucepan. Add the sugar and bring to a boil over medium-high heat, stirring. Continue to cook, stirring, until a syrup forms and the liquid is reduced by about half, 3–4 minutes. Remove from the heat and let cool.

Fill a bowl with water and add the lemon juice. Cut the apples lengthwise into quarters, and core the quarters. Place in the acidulated water to prevent discoloring. Using the julienne attachment on a mandoline, julienne the apples, and return them to the acidulated water. Alternatively, julienne with a knife.

In a bowl, combine the crabmeat, olive oil, vinegar, 2 tablespoons of the chives, the salt, black pepper, and cayenne. Pat dry half of the apples and add them to the bowl. Squeeze 2 teaspoons juice from the reserved grapefruit segments into the bowl. Turn gently to mix, being careful not to shred the crab.

To serve, divide the crab salad evenly among 8 salad plates, mounding it on each plate. Pat dry the remaining apples and divide them evenly among the salads, arranging them in a small stack on top. Spoon about 2 teaspoons of the grapefruit coulis in a thin line around the edge of each salad. To finish, sprinkle the remaining 1 tablespoon chives evenly over the salads.

1 grapefruit

2 teaspoons sugar

Juice of 1 lemon

2 Granny Smith apples

1 lb (500 g) fresh-cooked lump crabmeat, picked over for cartilage and shell fragments

3 tablespoons extra-virgin olive oil

1½ tablespoons white wine vinegar or Champagne vinegar

3 tablespoons minced fresh chives

½ teaspoon fine sea salt

½ teaspoon freshly ground black pepper

Pinch of cayenne pepper

SERVES 8

FRISÉE, ENDIVE, AND WATERCRESS SALAD WITH ROQUEFORT

To make the vinaigrette, in a small bowl, whisk together the vinegar, walnut oil, and honey. Stir in the pear. Season to taste with salt and pepper. Let stand at room temperature for at least 30 minutes or up to 4 hours.

In a large bowl, combine the frisée, endive, and watercress. Whisk the vinaigrette, drizzle it over the greens, and toss to coat the leaves well. Cut the Roquefort cheese into 6 slices. To serve, divide the greens evenly among chilled individual plates and top each with a slice of Roquefort. Serve at once.

The beauty of cheese in salads

Cheese adds flavor and protein to any salad. Blue cheeses, such as Gorgonzola or Roquefort, pair nicely with bitter greens and fruit, especially apples and pears. Feta is fantastic with romaine and spinach (add tomatoes and olives for a Greek mix); goat cheese works well with arugula (rocket), watercress, and Bibb lettuce; and Parmesan shavings add nutty flavor to any green.

Pear Vinaigrette

2 tablespoons Champagne vinegar

6 tablespoons (3 fl oz/90 ml) toasted walnut oil

1/2 teaspoon honey

1 firm but ripe pear such as Anjou or Bartlett (Williams'), peeled, cored, and cut into 1/4-inch (6-mm) dice

Salt and freshly ground pepper

1 head frisée, cored and torn into bite-sized pieces

2 heads Belgian endive (chicory/witloof), cored and cut lengthwise into narrow strips

1 bunch young, tender watercress, tough stems removed

6 oz (185 g) Roquefort cheese

SERVES 6

SHRIMP, SCALLOPS, AND STUFFED SQUID

Holidays are prime time for seafood feasts, from Dungeness crab to oyster bisque and oysters on the half shell. This luscious dish, featuring a trio of shellfish, is fabulous for an Italian-inspired gathering. You can stuff and refrigerate the squid several hours before cooking, and make the sauce the morning of the dinner.

Peel and devein the shrimp. In a bowl, combine the shrimp with ¼ cup (2 fl oz/60 ml) of the olive oil, the lemon juice, garlic, red pepper flakes, 1 teaspoon salt, and ½ teaspoon black pepper. Cover and refrigerate for 1 hour.

Preheat the broiler (grill). Remove the shrimp from the marinade, reserving the marinade, and lay them on a broiler pan. Broil (grill) 4–5 inches (10–13 cm) from the heat source, brushing twice with the marinade, until opaque throughout, 5–7 minutes. Transfer to a warmed platter and sprinkle with the parsley.

To make the scallops, dry well and season with salt and pepper. In a large frying pan over medium-high heat, melt the butter with the 2½ teaspoons olive oil. When hot, add the scallops and sear, turning once, until golden, about 30 seconds on each side. Pour in the wine and scrape up any browned bits. Add the vinegar and turn the scallops once more to cook through, about 1 minute total. Transfer to a warmed platter.

To make the stuffed squid, pat the whole bodies dry and mince the tentacles; set aside.

In a large saucepan over medium heat, warm 2 tablespoons of the olive oil. Add the shallots and sauté until translucent, about 4 minutes. Add half of the basil and the tomatoes and their juice and cook, stirring occasionally, until thick, about 20 minutes. Season with salt and pepper and stir in the remaining basil. Set aside.

In a frying pan over medium-high heat, heat 2 tablespoons of the olive oil. Add the onion and sauté until nearly translucent, about 2 minutes. Add the spinach and stir until wilted, about 2 minutes. Add the tentacles and bread crumbs and stir until the tentacles are opaque and the crumbs are lightly golden, about 4 minutes longer. Stir in the prosciutto, season with salt and pepper, and let cool. Pack 2–3 teaspoons into each squid body and close with a toothpick.

In a large frying pan over medium heat, warm the remaining 2 tablespoons olive oil. When hot, add the stuffed squid in a single layer and sauté, turning as needed, just until opaque, 4–5 minutes. Transfer to a warmed platter. Reheat the sauce and pour over the squid, serving the extra alongside. Serve all the seafood at once on a large platter.

36 large shrimp (prawns)

10 tablespoons (5 fl oz/160 ml) plus 2½ teaspoons olive oil

3 tablespoons lemon juice

2 cloves garlic, minced

¼ teaspoon red pepper flakes

Salt and freshly ground black pepper

2 teaspoons chopped fresh flat-leaf (Italian) parsley

18 sea scallops

1 teaspoon unsalted butter

⅔ cup (3 fl oz/80 ml) dry white wine

1 teaspoon balsamic vinegar

18 small squid, each 3–4 inches (7.5–10 cm) long, cleaned

2 large shallots, minced

¼ cup (⅓ oz/10 g) minced fresh basil

1 can (28 oz/875 g) plum (Roma) tomatoes, coarsely chopped, with juice

1 yellow onion, minced

4 cups (8 oz/250 g) chopped spinach

¼ cup (½ oz/15 g) fresh bread crumbs

¼ cup (2 oz/60 g) minced prosciutto

SERVES 6

BAKED GNOCCHI WITH TALEGGIO, PANCETTA, AND SAGE

You can also make this recipe using 1 lb (500 g) of tube-shaped dried pasta, such as penne. For a slightly less rich option, substitute fontina or Asiago cheese for the Taleggio. Packages of readymade and vacuum-packed gnocchi are sold in the fresh pasta section of most supermarkets.

Preheat the oven to 375°F (190°C). Butter four 7-inch (18-cm) shallow oval baking dishes.

Cook the gnocchi according to the package directions. Drain and set aside.

Lay the pancetta pieces in a single layer in a cold large frying pan. Place the pan over medium heat and cook until the pancetta starts to brown, about 2 minutes. Using a spatula, turn the pancetta pieces over and cook until browned, about 2 minutes longer. Remove from the heat and stir in the sage, gnocchi, half-and-half, and Taleggio.

Transfer the gnocchi mixture to the prepared baking dishes, dividing evenly. Sprinkle the tops with the bread crumbs and season with a few grinds of pepper. (The gnocchi can be prepared up to this point, cooled to room temperature, covered with plastic wrap, and refrigerated for up to 24 hours. Remove from the refrigerator 30 minutes before baking.)

Bake the gnocchi until golden, about 15 minutes. Serve hot, directly from the oven.

Comfort food for the winter months

A warm, gooey, oven-baked pasta with cheese is an easy crowd pleaser for dinner. Pair with a tossed green salad and a dry, medium-bodied Italian red wine, such as Chianti, Sangiovese, or Barbera.

2 tablespoons unsalted butter

2 packages (13 oz/410 g each) fresh gnocchi

¼ lb (125 g) sliced pancetta, cut into ½-inch (12-mm) pieces

2 tablespoons chopped fresh sage

1½ cups (12 fl oz/375 ml) half-and-half (half cream)

½ lb (250 g) Taleggio cheese, rind removed, cut into ¼-inch (6-mm) cubes

¼ cup (1 oz/30 g) toasted bread crumbs

Freshly ground pepper

SERVES 4

BAKED HAM WITH HONEY-PORT GLAZE

An 8-lb ham is the perfect size for a holiday dinner party. A bone-in ham offers more succulent flavor than a boneless one. To carve it, use a long carving knife to cut all the way around the bone, then cut the ham into slices.

Position a rack in the lower third of the oven and preheat to 325°F (165°C).

Using a sharp knife, score the fat on the upper half of the ham in a diamond pattern, cutting about ¼ inch (6 mm) deep. Place the ham, fat side up, on a rack in a shallow roasting pan. Roast for 1¼ hours.

In a small bowl, mix together the brown sugar, honey, and mustard. Pat half of the sugar mixture over the scored surface of the ham. Stir the Port into the remaining mixture. Continue to roast the ham, basting several times with the Port mixture, until the ham is glazed and shiny, about 1 hour longer.

Transfer the ham to a cutting board and tent loosely with aluminum foil. Let stand for 15 minutes or longer before carving.

1 fully cooked bone-in 8-lb (4-kg) ham

½ cup (3½ oz/105 g) firmly packed light brown sugar

¼ cup (3 oz/90 g) honey

2 teaspoons dry mustard

¾ cup (6 fl oz/180 ml) Port

SERVES 8–10

BOURBON-GLAZED HAM

A whole ham, glistening with a sugary glaze, forms a striking centerpiece for a holiday buffet. Slice the ham or cook a spiral-cut ham, so guests can serve themselves. Pair it with seared greens, roast potatoes, and caramelized onions on the side.

Preheat the oven to 325°F (165°C). Line a shallow roasting pan with aluminum foil and set a roasting rack in the pan. Cut away and discard any skin from the ham and trim the fat to ½ inch (12 mm) thick. Place the ham, fat side up, on the rack in the roasting pan. Roast until the ham is fully warmed through and an instant-read thermometer inserted into the thickest part of the ham (but not touching bone) registers 140°F (60°C), 3–3½ hours.

Remove the ham from the oven. Raise the oven temperature to 425°F (220°C). In a bowl, combine the brown sugar and bourbon and mix to make a paste. Score the fat on the upper half of the ham in a diamond pattern, cutting about ¼ inch (6 mm) deep. Rub the paste over the surface, then poke the cloves into random intersections of the diamonds. Return the ham to the oven and bake, basting several times with the pan juices, until the surface is shiny and beginning to brown, 15–20 minutes.

Transfer the ham to a cutting board and tent loosely with aluminum foil. Let stand for 20–30 minutes. Remove the cloves. Carve half of the ham and arrange on a warmed platter. Carve the remaining ham as needed.

1 fully cooked bone-in whole ham, about 20 lb (10 kg)

2½ cups (17½ oz/545 g) firmly packed dark brown sugar

⅓ cup (3 fl oz/80 ml) bourbon

15–20 whole cloves

SERVES 20–24

STANDING RIB ROAST WITH GARLIC-PEPPERCORN CRUST

Multicolored mixtures of peppercorns, sold in many markets, make a milder crust than black peppercorns alone do. When buying the roast, ask for a butcher's cut, with the bones separated but tied back on, which will add flavor during roasting and ease during carving. While the roast is resting, you can bake the Herbed Yorkshire Pudding (page 276).

In a mortar and using a pestle, crush the garlic and sea salt together to form a paste. Alternatively, crush together in a bowl with the bottom of a wooden spoon, or use a mini food processor. Add the peppercorns, thyme, paprika, and olive oil and mix to form a paste. Rub the paste all over the roast, coating it well. Cover loosely with aluminum foil and let stand at room temperature for 30 minutes.

Preheat the oven to 450°F (230°C).

Place the roast, bone side down, in a large roasting pan and roast for 30 minutes. Baste with the pan juices and reduce the oven temperature to 350°F (180°C). Continue to roast until an instant-read thermometer inserted into the thickest part of the meat (but not touching bone) registers 120°F (49°C) for rare, about 1 hour longer; or 125°–130°F (52°–54°C) for medium-rare, about 1¼ hours longer.

Transfer the roast to a carving board and tent loosely with aluminum foil. Let rest for

20–30 minutes before carving. While the roast is resting, skim off ¼ cup (2 fl oz/60 ml) of the fat from the pan and discard the rest. Combine the fat with some of the pan drippings and reserve to make the Yorkshire pudding (page 276).

If desired, make a sauce for the roast: Place the roasting pan with the remaining drippings on the stove top over medium-high heat and add the wine and up to 1 cup (8 fl oz/250 ml) water. Bring to a boil, stirring and scraping up any browned bits from the pan bottom. Cook until the sauce is thickened and reduced to about 1½ cups (12 fl oz/375 ml), 8–10 minutes. Strain through a fine-mesh sieve into a saucepan until ready to serve.

To serve, carve the roast into slices ¼–½ inch (6–12 mm) thick. Place the slices on a warmed platter and drizzle them with a little of the pan sauce. Serve at once.

4 cloves garlic, coarsely chopped

1½ tablespoons coarse sea salt

1 tablespoon freshly ground medium-coarse mixed peppercorns or black peppercorns

1 tablespoon fresh thyme leaves, minced

2 teaspoons paprika

2 teaspoons extra-virgin olive oil

1 butcher's-cut standing rib roast, 10–12 lb (5–6 kg), with 5 ribs

1 cup (8 fl oz/250 ml) Zinfandel, Merlot, or other dry red wine combined with ½ cup (4 fl oz/125 ml) Port (optional)

SERVES 8–10

BRAISED SHORT RIBS

Bone-in short ribs are delicious when cooked slowly in the oven. If short ribs are unavailable, ask the butcher to cut down full-sized ribs. The flavor of the dish intensifies if cooked a day ahead and reheated. To round out the menu, serve these ribs with polenta or a root vegetable gratin and a spicy fruit compote for dessert.

Put the ribs in a large bowl. In a cup, mix together 2 teaspoons each of the salt and pepper, the 1 tablespoon thyme leaves, and the paprika. Rub the seasonings all over the ribs. Cover and let stand for 2–4 hours (refrigerate if longer than 2 hours).

Preheat the oven to 325°F (165°C). In a Dutch oven or large, heavy pot with a lid, warm the olive oil over medium-high heat. Working in batches to avoid crowding, add the ribs in a single layer and cook, turning as needed, until browned on all sides and on the ends, about 5 minutes for each batch. Transfer to a bowl and set aside.

Pour off all but 2 tablespoons of the fat in the pot and return to medium-high heat. Stir in the onion and carrots and cook, stirring often, until the onion has softened, about 2 minutes. Stir in the garlic, then sprinkle the vegetables with the flour. Continue to cook, stirring, until the flour is lightly browned, about 2 minutes. Pour in the wine, scraping up any browned bits

on the bottom of the pot. Continue to stir, adding 1½ cups (12 fl oz/375 ml) water, the beef stock, tomato paste, vinegar, bay leaf, thyme sprigs, and the remaining 2 teaspoons each salt and pepper. Return the ribs and any collected juices to the pot and spoon the liquid over the ribs.

Cover, place in the oven, and cook for 1 hour. Uncover, stir the meat, re-cover, and continue to cook until the meat has nearly fallen off the bone and can easily be cut with a fork and knife, 2–2½ hours. Remove from the oven and skim off and discard the fat from the surface. (The ribs can be braised up to 1 day in advance. Remove from the heat, let cool, cover the pot, and refrigerate. The next day, remove from the refrigerator, lift off and discard any fat that has solidified on the surface, and reheat on the stove top over low heat for 30 minutes, stirring occasionally.)

Transfer to a deep platter, discarding the thyme sprigs and bay leaf. Garnish with the remaining fresh thyme leaves and serve at once.

4½ lb (2.25 kg) bone-in beef short ribs

4 teaspoons salt

4 teaspoons freshly ground pepper

1 tablespoon fresh thyme leaves plus 5 or 6 sprigs and extra leaves for garnish

1 tablespoon paprika

3 tablespoons extra-virgin olive oil

1 yellow onion, chopped

2 carrots, peeled and sliced on the diagonal

3 cloves garlic, chopped

1 tablespoon all-purpose (plain) flour

1½ cups (12 fl oz/375 ml) dry red wine such as Syrah or Merlot

2 cups (16 fl oz/500 ml) beef stock or reduced-sodium beef broth

1½ tablespoons tomato paste

2 teaspoons balsamic vinegar

1 bay leaf

SERVES 6–8

BEEF TENDERLOIN WITH SHALLOT AND SYRAH REDUCTION

The source of the filet mignon, the tenderloin is the tenderest cut of beef. It needs only relatively brief cooking. The Syrah reduction, made from the flavorful pan juices, is quickly prepared while the roast rests. Serve this classic dish with a full-bodied red wine, such as Cabernet Sauvignon.

Preheat the oven to 450°F (230°C).

Rub the beef all over with the olive oil, then rub on the thyme, salt, and pepper.

Place the roast on a rack in a shallow roasting pan just large enough to accommodate it. Roast until an instant-read thermometer inserted into the thickest part of the meat registers 115°–120°F (46°–49°C) for rare, about 20 minutes; 125°–130°F (52°–54°C) for medium-rare, about 25 minutes; or 130°–140°F (54°–60°C) for medium, about 30 minutes.

Transfer the roast to a carving board and tent loosely with aluminum foil. Let rest for about 15 minutes before serving.

Meanwhile, remove the rack from the roasting pan and place the pan on the stove top over medium heat. Add the shallots and sauté, stirring them into the pan juices, until translucent, about 2 minutes. Add the wine a little at a time, stirring and scraping up any browned bits from the bottom of the pan. Continue to cook until the wine is reduced by nearly half. Stir in the butter. When the butter has melted, remove from the heat and cover to keep warm.

To serve, cut the beef into slices 1/2 inch (12 mm) thick. Arrange the slices on a warmed platter and drizzle with the sauce. Serve at once.

1 beef tenderloin,
2¹/₂–3 lb (1.25–1.5 kg)

2 tablespoons
extra-virgin olive oil

2 teaspoons minced
fresh thyme

1¹/₂ teaspoons fine sea salt

1 teaspoon freshly
ground pepper

2 tablespoons
minced shallots

1 cup (8 fl oz/250 ml) Syrah

2¹/₂ tablespoons
unsalted butter

SERVES 8

HERBED YORKSHIRE PUDDING

Preheat the oven to 400°F (200°C). In a small saucepan over medium-high heat, warm the reserved beef fat. In a bowl, whisk together the flour, salt, parsley, and chives. In another bowl, whisk together the eggs and the milk, then whisk in the flour mixture until blended.

Distribute the heated beef fat among 12 nonstick standard muffin cups, then pour in the batter. Bake for 15 minutes. Reduce the oven temperature to 350°F (180°C) and continue to bake until the pudding is puffed and golden brown, about 15 minutes longer. Remove from the oven and, using a table knife, loosen the sides of each pudding to remove them from the pan. Serve at once with the rib roast.

¼ cup (2 fl oz/60 ml) reserved fat from the beef roasting pan (page 271)

1 cup (5 oz/155 g) all-purpose (plain) flour

1½ teaspoons fine sea salt

½ cup (¾ oz/20 g) each minced fresh flat-leaf (Italian) parsley and chives

4 large eggs

1½ cups (12 fl oz/375 ml) whole milk

SERVES 8–10

BRAISED BRUSSELS SPROUTS WITH SAGE

Cut the base off each sprout and peel away as many of the leaves as you can. Cut the tightly wrapped inner core lengthwise into quarters. Put the leaves and quarters in a bowl with water to cover. Using your hands, transfer the sprouts to a large sauté pan. Add 1 cup (8 fl oz/250 ml) water, bring to a boil over medium-high heat, cover, reduce the heat to low, and cook until tender when pierced with a fork, about 15 minutes. Drain and rinse under cold running water.

Wipe the pan dry. Add the butter, olive oil, and sage. Cook over medium heat for 3 minutes. Do not brown the sage. Add the Brussels sprouts, salt, and pepper and sauté until the leaves glisten, about 10 minutes. Taste and adjust the seasoning. Serve hot.

2 lb (1 kg) Brussels sprouts

5 tablespoons (2½ oz/75 g) unsalted butter

3 tablespoons olive oil

¼ cup (⅓ oz/10 g) chopped fresh sage leaves

1½ teaspoons salt

1 teaspoon freshly ground pepper

SERVES 8–10

POLENTA WITH WHITE CHEDDAR

Put 8 cups (64 fl oz/2 l) water in a large saucepan and add 1½ teaspoons of the salt. Bring to a boil over high heat. Add the polenta in a slow, steady stream, stirring constantly. Reduce the heat to low and cook, stirring frequently, until the polenta pulls away from the sides of the pan, 35–40 minutes.

Stir in the butter, all but ¼ cup (1 oz/30 g) of the cheese, the remaining 1 teaspoon salt, and the pepper and cook until the butter and cheese have melted into the polenta, 3–4 minutes longer.

Spoon the polenta into a large warmed bowl and sprinkle with the remaining ¼ cup cheese and some pepper. Serve at once.

2½ teaspoons salt

1½ cups (10½ oz/330 g) polenta

3 tablespoons unsalted butter

1¾ cups (7 oz/220 g) finely shredded white Cheddar cheese

1 teaspoon freshly ground pepper, plus more for sprinkling

SERVES 6–8

SWISS CHARD GRATIN

Position a rack 6 inches (15 cm) from the heat source and preheat the broiler (grill). Oil a flameproof baking dish about 12 inches (30 cm) in diameter.

In a large saucepan, combine the chard, 1 teaspoon of the salt, and water to cover by 4 inches (10 cm). Bring to a boil over high heat, reduce the heat to medium, and cook until the stems are tender, 15–20 minutes. Remove from the heat, rinse under cold water, squeeze dry, and chop coarsely. (The chard can be prepared up to 6 hours in advance.)

In a large frying pan over medium heat, warm the oil. Stir in the garlic, chard, remaining ½ teaspoon salt, and the pepper. Transfer to the prepared dish and sprinkle with the cheeses. Broil (grill) until golden on top, about 5 minutes. Serve hot.

16 large Swiss chard leaves (about 2 bunches), tough stems trimmed

1½ teaspoons salt

2 tablespoons extra-virgin olive oil

1 clove garlic, minced

¼ teaspoon freshly ground pepper

¼ cup (1 oz/30 g) finely shredded Gruyère cheese

¼ cup (1 oz/30 g) freshly grated Parmesan cheese

SERVES 6–8

CREAMY GRATIN OF WINTER VEGETABLES

Parsnips, rutabagas, and turnips are combined with coarsely mashed potatoes, then topped with cheese, gratinéed, and transformed into a delicious winter-warming dish. The root vegetables add texture while enhancing the background flavor of the potatoes.

Preheat the oven to 350°F (180°C). Lightly butter a 12-inch (30-cm) flameproof gratin dish.

Peel the parsnips, rutabagas, turnip, and potatoes and cut into 1-inch (2.5-cm) cubes. Put the vegetables in a stockpot, add water to cover by 4–5 inches (10–13 cm), and add the coarse sea salt. Bring to a boil over high heat, reduce the heat to medium, and cook, uncovered, until the vegetables are easily pierced with a fork, about 25 minutes.

Drain the vegetables well and transfer to a large bowl. Sprinkle with the fine sea salt and pepper and turn several times.

In a saucepan over medium heat, combine the half-and-half, whole milk, and 2 tablespoons butter and heat, stirring occasionally, just until tiny bubbles form along the edge of the pan.

Pour half of the milk mixture over the vegetables and mash coarsely with a potato masher. When the milk mixture has been absorbed, add the remaining milk mixture and 3 tablespoons of the parsley. Mash coarsely again until well blended. Spoon the mashed mixture into the prepared gratin dish, smoothing the surface. Sprinkle the cheeses on top. Cut the remaining 1 teaspoon butter into bits and dot the top.

Bake until bubbles begin to form along the edges and the top begins to turn golden, 15–20 minutes. Preheat the broiler (grill) and broil (grill) until the top is golden, 3–4 minutes. Remove from the broiler and sprinkle with the remaining 1 tablespoon parsley. Serve hot.

3 large parsnips

2 small rutabagas

1 medium turnip

3 Yukon gold potatoes

1 tablespoon coarse sea salt or kosher salt

2 teaspoons fine sea salt

1 teaspoon freshly ground pepper

1/2 cup (4 fl oz/125 ml) half-and-half (half cream)

1/2 cup (4 fl oz/125 ml) whole milk

2 tablespoons plus 1 teaspoon unsalted butter

4 tablespoons (1/3 oz/10 g) minced fresh flat-leaf (Italian) parsley

3 tablespoons grated Parmesan cheese

3 tablespoons finely shredded Gruyère cheese

SERVES 8–10

ROASTED CAULIFLOWER WITH GREEN OLIVES

This dish tastes best at room temperature, making it ideal for entertaining. To save preparation time, look for large green olives that have already been pitted, sold in glass jars or available at supermarket olive bars.

Preheat the oven to 400°F (200°C). Lightly oil a 12-by-17-inch (30-by-43-cm) nonstick rimmed baking sheet.

Cut the cauliflower head in half, slicing through the core. Using a sharp paring knife, remove the core from each half and discard. Cut the cauliflower into small florets, each about ½ inch (12 mm) in diameter.

In a bowl, combine the cauliflower, olives, olive oil, salt, and pepper and toss until the cauliflower and olives are evenly coated. Transfer to the prepared baking sheet and spread in a single layer. Roast the cauliflower and olives for 10 minutes. Stir to toss and continue to roast until the florets are lightly golden, 10–12 minutes longer. Remove from the oven. Sprinkle with the parsley and bread crumbs and toss to combine. Let cool to room temperature. (The cauliflower and olives can be roasted up to 1 day in advance, covered, refrigerated, and brought to room temperature before serving.)

To serve, mound the cauliflower and olives in the center of a platter or shallow serving bowl.

1 large head cauliflower, about 2 lb (1 kg)

1 cup (4 oz/125 g) pitted large green olives, quartered

¼ cup (2 fl oz/60 ml) olive oil

¼ teaspoon kosher salt

¼ teaspoon freshly ground pepper

2 tablespoons chopped fresh flat-leaf (Italian) parsley

⅓ cup (½ oz/45 g) store-bought seasoned croutons, ground to crumbs in a food processor

SERVES 8

ROASTED POTATOES WITH SEA SALT

Long, slow roasting in olive oil with a sprinkling of sea salt produces potatoes with a slightly crunchy skin and a creamy interior. Instead of using sage sprigs, you can substitute fresh rosemary.

Preheat the oven to 350°F (180°C). Arrange the potatoes in a single layer in a large roasting pan. Pour the oil over them and turn to coat well. Sprinkle with the salt, turn again, and tuck in the sage sprigs. Roast until the skins are slightly wrinkled and the insides are tender and creamy when pierced with the tip of a sharp knife, about 1½ hours.

6 lb (3 kg) baby red potatoes, each 1½–2 inches (4–5 cm) in diameter

⅓ cup (3 fl oz/80 ml) extra-virgin olive oil

1½ tablespoons coarse sea salt

15–20 large fresh sage sprigs

SERVES 12–14

CHOCOLATE FRANGELICO TRUFFLES

Homemade truffles are easy to make and can be prepared up to 2 weeks in advance. In this recipe, they receive a double dose of hazelnut flavoring, in the liqueur and in the nut coating. Keep the truffles in the freezer until just before serving. For a fuller, dark chocolate taste, use bittersweet chocolate in place of the semisweet.

Cut the chocolate into 1-inch (2.5-cm) pieces. Place in the top pan of a double boiler set over (but not touching) gently simmering water. Stir as the chocolate melts. When it is melted, stir in the cream, mixing well.

Remove the top pan from the heat and let the chocolate cool until nearly firm, 2–3 hours. Stir the Frangelico into the cooled chocolate.

Line a tray or baking sheet with parchment (baking) paper or aluminum foil. Using a melon baller, scoop out rounds of chocolate, placing them on the tray. When all the chocolate has been used, cover the chocolate balls with aluminum foil and place the tray in the freezer for at least 30 minutes or for up to 2 weeks.

A few hours before serving, remove the truffles from the freezer. Place the cocoa powder in a small shallow bowl and the ground nuts in a second bowl. Roll the frozen balls first in the cocoa and then in the hazelnuts, coating them evenly each time and handling them as little as possible. As each ball is coated, return it to the tray. Then return the tray to the freezer.

About 15 minutes before serving, remove the tray from the freezer and arrange the truffles on a serving platter.

8 oz (250 g) semisweet (plain) chocolate

1/2 cup (4 fl oz/125 ml) heavy (double) cream

2–3 teaspoons Frangelico liqueur

1/2 cup (1 1/2 oz/45 g) unsweetened cocoa powder

1/2 cup (2 oz/60 g) finely ground hazelnuts (filberts)

MAKES ABOUT 40 TRUFFLES; SERVES 14–16

APPLE-GINGER TART WITH CIDER-BOURBON SAUCE

A warm bourbon sauce is the perfect complement to this streusel-topped apple tart. It can be made a day in advance and reheated over low heat just before serving. You can use Anjou or Bosc pears in place of the apples; decrease the baking time by 15 minutes.

Preheat the oven to 425°F (220°C).

To make the pastry, in a food processor, combine the flour, butter, and confectioners' sugar. Pulse until fine crumbs form. Measure out 1/3 cup (3/4 oz/20 g) of the crumb mixture and set aside.

Pat the remaining crumb mixture evenly on the bottom and up the sides of an 11-inch (28-cm) tart pan with a removable bottom. Refrigerate or freeze the tart shell for 10 minutes. Bake until the tart shell just begins to brown, about 6 minutes. Let cool completely on a wire rack.

To make the filling, halve and core the unpeeled apples and then thinly slice. In a small bowl, mix together the reserved crumb mixture and the brown sugar. In a large bowl, combine the apple slices, granulated sugar, lemon juice, ginger, and cinnamon. Toss to coat the apples. Pile the filling into the cooled pastry shell and smooth into an even layer. Sprinkle with the brown sugar mixture.

Bake for 15 minutes. Reduce the oven temperature to 375°F (190°C) and continue to bake until the apples are tender when pierced with a knife, 45–50 minutes longer. Cover the top with aluminum foil during the last 30 minutes to prevent the top from browning too much. Transfer to a wire rack and let cool.

To make the sauce, in a small saucepan over medium heat, combine the brown sugar and cornstarch, stirring to remove any lumps. Stir in the apple cider and salt. Raise the heat to medium-high and bring to a boil, stirring constantly. Cook until thickened, about 4 minutes. Reduce the heat to medium, stir in the butter and bourbon, and simmer just until blended and the butter is melted.

Cut the tart into wedges to serve. Drizzle a little of the hot sauce over each wedge.

Pastry

1 1/4 cups (6 1/2 oz/200 g) all-purpose (plain) flour

10 tablespoons (5 oz/155 g) cold unsalted butter

2 tablespoons confectioners' (icing) sugar

Filling

8 Granny Smith or Golden Delicious apples, about 3 lb (1.5 kg) total weight

1/3 cup (2 1/2 oz/75 g) firmly packed light brown sugar

1/4 cup (2 oz/60 g) granulated sugar

3 tablespoons fresh lemon juice

6 tablespoons (2 oz/60 g) finely chopped crystallized ginger

1 teaspoon ground cinnamon

Cider-Bourbon Sauce

1 cup (7 oz/220 g) firmly packed light brown sugar

2 tablespoons cornstarch (cornflour)

2 cups (16 fl oz/500 ml) apple cider

Pinch of salt

1/4 cup (2 oz/60 g) unsalted butter

1/2 cup (4 fl oz/125 ml) bourbon

SERVES 8–10

STEAMED FIG PUDDING

Steamed puddings are a traditional holiday dessert in England, and those made with dried figs are an especially classic variety. They can vary in texture and taste. This version has the flavor of a rich bread pudding. Each serving is enhanced with a drizzle of dense syrup made from the fig poaching liquid and a dollop of whipped cream.

Butter a 7-cup (1½-qt/1.5-l) pudding mold.

In a small saucepan over medium-high heat, combine the figs, currants, and 2 cups (16 fl oz/500 ml) water and bring to a boil. Reduce the heat to low and simmer, uncovered, until the figs are tender but still hold their shape, about 20 minutes. Remove from the heat and let stand in the cooking liquid. Meanwhile, place the toasted walnuts in a food processor and pulse to grind finely.

Tear the bread into pea-sized crumbs. In a large bowl, whisk together the bread crumbs, walnuts, and flour. Using a slotted spoon, transfer the figs and currants to another bowl. Reserve the cooking liquid. Halve 8–10 of the figs lengthwise and press them, cut side down, in a decorative pattern in the prepared mold. Coarsely chop the remaining figs; set aside.

In a bowl, using an electric mixer on medium-high speed, beat together the butter and brown sugar until fluffy. Add the eggs one at a time, beating well after each addition. Beat in the milk and vanilla. Stir in the currants and chopped figs. Fold half of the flour mixture into the egg mixture. Fold in the remaining flour mixture.

Pour the batter into the mold and fasten the lid. Place the mold on a rack in a large pot and pour in boiling water to reach halfway up the sides of the mold. Bring to a boil over high heat. Reduce the heat to medium-low, cover the pot, and boil for 2 hours, being careful not to let it boil over and replenishing the water as needed to maintain the original level. The pudding should slowly steam.

Remove the mold from the water and let stand for 15 minutes. Remove the lid, invert the mold onto a platter, and tap gently to release the steamed pudding.

Using an electric mixer on medium speed, whip the cream until soft peaks form. Slowly add the granulated sugar while continuing to whip until stiff peaks form. At the same time, bring the reserved fig liquid to a boil over high heat and cook until reduced to ½ cup (4 fl oz/125 ml) syrup, about 5 minutes.

To serve, cut the pudding into 1-inch (2.5-cm) wedges, drizzle some syrup alongside, and top with the whipped cream.

1½ cups (8 oz/250 g) dried figs, tough stem ends trimmed

½ cup (3 oz/90 g) dried currants

1 cup (4 oz/125 g) walnuts, toasted

8 slices white sandwich bread, crusts removed

1¼ cups (6½ oz/200 g) all-purpose (plain) flour

7 tablespoons (3½ oz/ 105 g) unsalted butter, at room temperature

½ cup (3½ oz/105 g) firmly packed dark brown sugar

3 large eggs

1 cup (8 fl oz/250 ml) whole milk

1 teaspoon vanilla extract

Boiling water as needed

1½ cups (12 fl oz/375 ml) heavy (double) cream

¼ cup (2 oz/60 g) granulated sugar

SERVES 8–10

WINTER COMPOTE WITH CLOVE BISCOTTI

The clove biscotti complement the sweet-tart poached fruits and can be dipped in the compote to soak up the tasty juices. If you want to serve purchased cookies, look for almond biscotti, which will be a nice match with the fruits. Serve the compote with freshly whipped cream, if desired.

To make the biscotti, preheat the oven to 350°F (180°C). Butter a baking sheet and dust with flour. In a large bowl, whisk together the flour, salt, chopped and ground walnuts, baking soda, and ground cloves. Make a well in the center and add the eggs, sugar, and clove extract. Using an electric mixer or a whisk, beat the eggs and sugar into the dry ingredients until a stiff, sticky dough forms. (If the dough remains too wet, add more flour.) With lightly floured hands, gather the dough into a ball, place on a lightly floured work surface, and knead until firm, 2–3 minutes. Divide into 2 or 3 equal portions. Using your palms, roll each portion into a log 1½–2 inches (4–5 cm) in diameter.

Place the logs on the prepared baking sheet, spacing them well apart. Bake until each log is light brown, about 25 minutes. Remove from the oven and let cool on the baking sheet for 10 minutes. Using a sharp knife, cut each log crosswise on the diagonal into 20–25 slices about ½ inch (12 mm) thick. Place the slices, cut side down, on the baking sheet, spacing them ½ inch (12 mm) apart (you will probably have to bake in batches). Bake until lightly golden on the underside, 7–8 minutes. Remove from the oven, turn the biscotti, and continue baking until faintly golden on the second side, 7–8 minutes longer. Remove from the oven and transfer the biscotti to wire racks to cool. (The biscotti can be made up to 5 days in advance and stored in an airtight container.)

To make the compote, in a saucepan, combine the pears, figs, cherries, wine, sugar, and star anise with 1 cup (8 fl oz/250 ml) water and bring to a boil over medium-high heat. Reduce the heat to low and simmer, uncovered, until the fruits are plump, 10–15 minutes. Remove from the heat and let stand for at least 30 minutes before serving. (The compote can be made up to 2 days in advance, covered, and refrigerated. Warm over low heat before serving.) Remove the star anise or keep to use as a garnish.

Serve the compote warm in individual bowls. Accompany with the biscotti.

Biscotti

1½ cups (7½ oz/235 g) all-purpose (plain) flour, plus 1–3 tablespoons more if needed

¼ teaspoon salt

¼ cup (1 oz/30 g) coarsely chopped walnuts

1½ cups (6 oz/185 g) finely ground walnuts

1 teaspoon baking soda (bicarbonate of soda)

½ teaspoon freshly ground cloves

3 large eggs

½ cup (4 oz/125 g) sugar

½ teaspoon clove extract

Compote

10 dried pear halves, cut in half lengthwise

16 dried figs, cut in half lengthwise

25 dried cherries

1 cup (8 fl oz/250 ml) sweet white wine such as muscat, Beaumes-de-Venise, or late-harvest Riesling

1 tablespoon sugar

1 whole star anise

SERVES 6–8

RICOTTA CHEESECAKE WITH BLOOD ORANGE GLAZE

Ricotta gives this cake an added creaminess, and garnet-hued blood orange marmalade makes a tangy and colorful topping. You can use any citrus marmalade for the glaze—seville orange, lemon, or Meyer lemon, which will give a slightly sweeter flavor.

Preheat the oven to 325°F (165°C).

To make the crust, in a food processor, finely chop the cookies and transfer to a bowl. Finely grind the walnuts with the sugar and add to the ground cookies. Add the melted butter and mix well until the dry ingredients are evenly moistened. Transfer the crumb mixture to a 9-inch (23-cm) springform pan and, using your fingers, cover the bottom and about 1½ inches (4 cm) up the sides of the pan. Bake until lightly browned, about 15 minutes. Let cool on a wire rack for 10 minutes, then place in the freezer. Reduce the oven temperature to 300°F (150°C).

To make the filling, in a blender or food processor, combine the cream cheese, ricotta, orange zest, sugar, vanilla, egg yolks, cream, and salt. Process until smooth, 1–2 minutes. Pour into a large bowl. In another bowl, using an electric mixer on high speed, beat the egg whites until stiff peaks form. Using a spatula, fold about ⅓ of the egg whites into the cheese mixture and stir to incorporate. Then, gently fold in the remaining egg whites just until incorporated.

Remove the crust from the freezer and pour the cheese mixture into it, smoothing the top. Bake for 30 minutes. Raise the oven temperature to 325°F (165°C) and continue to bake until the surface is golden and the edges are firm but the center still jiggles, 30–35 minutes longer. Turn off the oven, open the oven door, and let the cheesecake cool in the oven for about 3 hours. The center will fall slightly. Cover with plastic wrap, being careful not to let the wrap touch the surface. Refrigerate for at least 12 hours or up to overnight.

To make the blood orange glaze, in a small saucepan over low heat, combine the marmalade and 2–3 tablespoons of water and heat, stirring occasionally, to melt the marmalade. Set aside until cool, then spread on top of the cheesecake, creating an even layer of glaze. Garnish with the orange zest. Release and remove the pan sides and place the cheesecake on a serving plate. To serve, cut into wedges with a sharp knife, dipping the knife into water and wiping it dry after each cut.

Crust

6 oz (185 g) gingersnap cookies

1¼ cups (5 oz/155 g) walnuts

¼ cup (2 oz/60 g) sugar

5 tablespoons (2½ oz/75 g) unsalted butter, melted

Filling

8 oz (250 g) cream cheese, at room temperature, cut into 4 pieces

7 oz (220 g) whole-milk ricotta, drained well

Grated zest of 1 orange

1 cup (8 oz/250 g) sugar

1 teaspoon vanilla extract

4 large eggs, separated

⅔ cup (5 fl oz/160 ml) heavy (double) cream

⅛ teaspoon salt

Blood Orange Glaze

½ cup (5 oz/155 g) blood orange or regular orange marmalade

Shredded zest of 1 orange

SERVES 8–10

GINGERBREAD WITH WHIPPED CREAM

Ginger in three forms triples the impact of this wonderfully spicy cake, a fresh alternative to more traditional gingerbread. You can top each slice with a dollop of whipped cream and a sprinkle of crystallized ginger, or frost the whole cake with the cream just before serving and scatter the ginger evenly over the top.

Preheat the oven to 350°F (180°C). Line a 12-by-17-inch (30-by-43-cm) half-sheet pan or two 7-by-11-by-1½-inch (18-by-28-by-4-cm) baking pans with parchment (baking) paper.

In a bowl, whisk together the flour, baking soda, salt, ground ginger, cinnamon, and allspice. In a large bowl, using an electric mixer on medium-high speed, beat the butter and brown sugar together until creamy. Beat in the egg. Add the molasses and fresh ginger and beat until well mixed, about 2 minutes. Beat in the flour mixture in 3 batches, alternating with the buttermilk in 2 batches. Using a rubber spatula, scrape the batter into the prepared pan(s).

Bake until a toothpick inserted in the center comes out clean, 25–30 minutes. Let cool in the pan on a wire rack for 10 minutes. Slip a knife or an icing spatula between the paper and the pan(s) and then gently invert the cake(s) onto the rack. (If making a large single sheet of gingerbread, place 2 or 3 racks together.) Peel off the paper, turn the cake(s) right side up, and let cool completely on the rack(s). Transfer the cooled cake(s) to a cutting board. Set aside until ready to serve.

Using the electric mixer on medium-high speed, beat the cream. Sprinkle in all of the confectioners' sugar and beat until soft peaks form. Cover and refrigerate until ready to serve the cake. Briefly beat the cream again with a whisk if there is any separation.

Cut the cake into triangles and arrange the triangles on a platter or pedestal. Top each serving with a dollop of whipped cream. Scatter the crystallized ginger over the cream and cakes and serve.

3 cups (15 oz/470 g) all-purpose (plain) flour

1 teaspoon baking soda (bicarbonate of soda)

½ teaspoon salt

1 tablespoon ground ginger

1 teaspoon ground cinnamon

1 teaspoon ground allspice

1 cup (8 oz/250 g) unsalted butter, at room temperature

1 cup (7 oz/220 g) firmly packed light brown sugar

1 large egg

1 cup (11 oz/345 g) light molasses

¼ cup (1½ oz/45 g) peeled and grated fresh ginger

1 cup (8 fl oz/250 ml) buttermilk

1½ cups (12 fl oz/375 ml) heavy (double) cream

6 tablespoons (1½ oz/45 g) confectioners' (icing) sugar

¾ cup (4½ oz/140 g) minced crystallized ginger

SERVES 12–14

spring menus

CASUAL DINNER • 4

Creamed Broccoli-Leek Soup, 43

Shredded Chicken Salad with Sherry Dressing, 44

Cheddar and Chive Biscuits, 60

Fruit Compote with Brown Sugar Cookies, 68

WINE PAIRING • Riesling / Merlot

CASUAL DINNER • 6 to 8

Campari and Orange Cocktails, 26

Fried Artichokes with Aioli, 32

Arugula, Fennel, and Orange Salad, 48

Lemon Risotto, 56

Lemon Pound Cake, 71

WINE PAIRING • Prosecco

CASUAL DINNER • 10 to 12

Sparkling Mint Lemonade, 25

Baby Spinach Salad with Parmesan and Papaya, 47

Mushroom-Stuffed Chicken with Spring Vegetables, 52

Strawberry-Rhubarb Galette, 63

WINE PAIRING • Chardonnay / Pinot Noir

ELEGANT DINNER • 6

Butter Lettuce and Herb Salad with Dijon Vinaigrette, 47

Roasted Fish with Chive Butter and Caviar, 51

Roasted Asparagus, 59

Chocolate Espresso Crèmes with Candied Citrus, 64

WINE PAIRING • Sauvignon Blanc / Rosé

ELEGANT DINNER • 6 to 8

Radishes with Butter and Sea Salt, 39

Boneless Leg of Lamb with Herbes de Provence, 55

Flageolet Beans with Oregano, 59

Lemon Custards with Lemon Verbena Cream, 67

WINE PAIRING • French Syrah / Grenache

COCKTAIL PARTY • 10 to 12

White Lillet Cocktails, 21

Mojitos, 22

Crostini with Fava Bean Spread and Mint, 31

Endive Tipped with Ahi and Green Peppercorns, 35

Oven-Roasted Pesto Shrimp Skewers, 36

Marinated Feta Cubes, 40

summer menus

CASUAL DINNER · 6 to 8

Mango-Guava Sparklers, 82

Caprese Salad, 107

Grilled Sausages and Portobellos, 120

Grilled Peaches with Toasted Almonds, 139

WINE PAIRING · Pinot Grigio / Merlot

CASUAL DINNER · 10 to 12

Cucumber-Lime Coolers, 81

Grilled Corn with Chipotle Butter, 128

Grilled Tomatillo Chicken Fajitas, 119

Ice Cream Sundaes, 136

ELEGANT DINNER · 6 to 8

Cucumber-Dill Soup, 104

Orzo Salad with Basil and Heirloom Tomatoes, 107

Pan-Seared Sea Bass with Herb Butter, 116

Plum Gratin with Honey-Lavender Cream, 143

WINE PAIRING · Albariño / Pinot Noir

ELEGANT DINNER · 6 to 8

Lobster Salad with Champagne Vinaigrette, 115

Lamb Brochettes with Mint Gremolata, 124

Cucumber Ribbons with Tomatoes, Ricotta
Salata, and Olives, 111

Apricot-Pistachio Tart, 132

WINE PAIRING · Rosé / Zinfandel

COCKTAIL PARTY · 8 to 10

Plum and Nectarine Sangria, 85

Citrus Caipirinhas, 81

Parmesan-Zucchini Frittata, 92

Shrimp, Cantaloupe, and Fresh Herb Skewers, 96

Grilled Calamari Skewers, 99

COCKTAIL PARTY · 12 to 14

Classic Margaritas, 89

Watermelon and Tequila Frescas, 82

Tenderloin and Heirloom Tomato Canapés, 100

Scallop Ceviche, 99

Corn Fritters with Romesco Sauce, 95

autumn menus

CASUAL DINNER • 4
Mâche, Radish, and Sugared Pecan Salad, 175

Grilled Halibut with Potato-Fennel Puree, 184

Apple-Pear Crisp, 211

WINE PAIRING • Sauvignon Blanc / Merlot

CASUAL DINNER • 6 to 8
Arugula Salad with Pecorino and Pine Nuts, 179

Black-Pepper Beef Tenderloin with Celery Root, 191

Brussels Sprouts with Pancetta and Onions, 208

Chocolate-Hazelnut Brownies with Ice Cream, 220

WINE PAIRING • Soave / Cabernet Sauvignon

THANKSGIVING DINNER • 10 to 12
Butternut Squash Soup, 172

Roast Turkey with Pan Gravy, 192

Apple, Celery, and Sourdough Stuffing, 203

Fresh Cranberry Relish, 196

Mashed Yukon Gold Potatoes, 199

Green Beans with Garlic, 200

Pumpkin Cheesecake, 219

WINE PAIRING • Chardonnay / Zinfandel

ELEGANT DINNER • 6 to 8
Roasted Almond and Date Spread, 164

Celery, Pear, and Toasted Hazelnut Salad, 176

Squash Ravioli with Brown Butter and Pecans, 187

Apple and Cranberry Galette, 212

WINE PAIRING • Viognier / Barbera

ELEGANT DINNER • 8
Gorgonzola Bruschetta with Figs, 160

Herbed Pork Tenderloin with Pancetta and Capers, 188

Wild Rice and Leek Pilaf, 204

Pear Tart Tatin with Brandied Cream, 215

WINE PAIRING • Rosé / Pinot Noir

COCKTAIL PARTY • 8 to 10
Grapefruit Martinis, 157

Cranberry Gin Fizz, 157

Spiced Nuts, 163

Crostini with Artichoke-Parmesan Spread, 163

Baked Brie with Pistachios and Dried Fruit, 168

Antipasto Platter, 167

winter menus

CASUAL DINNER · 6

Campari and Soda, 234

Arugula, Radicchio, and Escarole Salad, 259

Shrimp, Scallops, and Stuffed Squid, 264

Ricotta Cheesecake with Blood Orange Glaze, 292

WINE PAIRING · Prosecco / Chianti

CASUAL DINNER · 8 to 10

Orange, Avocado, and Fennel Salad, 259

Baked Ham with Honey-Port Glaze, 268

Creamy Gratin of Winter Vegetables, 280

Apple-Ginger Tart with Cider-Bourbon Sauce, 287

WINE PAIRING · Chardonnay / Pinot Noir

ELEGANT DINNER · 6

Winter Citrus Spritzers, 229

Frisée, Endive, and Watercress Salad with Roquefort, 263

Braised Short Ribs, 272

Polenta with White Cheddar, 279

Winter Compote with Clove Biscotti, 291

WINE PAIRING · Petit Syrah

ELEGANT DINNER · 8

Pomegranate Sparklers, 229

Golden Beet Soup with Crème Fraîche, 255

Standing Rib Roast with Garlic-Peppercorn Crust, 271

Herbed Yorkshire Pudding, 276

Swiss Chard Gratin, 279

Steamed Fig Pudding, 288

WINE PAIRING · Cabernet Sauvignon

COCKTAIL PARTY · 10

Champagne with Liqueur, 234

Lemon Vodka Martinis, 230

Oysters on the Half Shell, 240

Brioche Rounds with Caviar, 243

Cucumber with Fresh Crab, 244

Chocolate Frangelico Truffles, 284

COCKTAIL PARTY · 12

Eggnog with Nutmeg and Cinnamon, 237

Hot Spiced Red Wine, 237

Rosemary Roasted Almonds, 248

Pecorino Gougères with Prosciutto, 247

Chicken Liver Mousse with Cornichons, 252

Roasted Lamb Chops with Rosemary and Sea Salt, 251

INDEX

FREE PRESS

A division of Simon & Schuster, Inc.
1230 Avenue of the Americas
New York, NY 10020

WILLIAMS-SONOMA, INC.
Founder and Vice-Chairman Chuck Williams

WELDON OWEN INC.
CEO and President Terry Newell
Senior VP, International Sales Stuart Laurence
VP, Sales and New Business Development Amy Kaneko
Director of Finance Mark Perrigo

VP and Publisher Hannah Rahill
Associate Publisher Amy Marr
Assistant Editor Julia Nelson

Associate Creative Director Emma Boys
Designer Lauren Charles

Production Director Chris Hemesath
Production Manager Michelle Duggan
Color Manager Teri Bell

Group Publisher, Bonnier Publishing Group John Owen

ENTERTAINING WITH THE SEASONS

Conceived and produced by Weldon Owen, Inc.
415 Jackson Street, Suite 200, San Francisco, CA 94111
Telephone: 415 291 0100 Fax: 415 291 8841
www.weldonowen.com

In collaboration with Williams-Sonoma, Inc.
3250 Van Ness Avenue, San Francisco, CA 94109

A WELDON OWEN PRODUCTION

Copyright © 2010 Weldon Owen, Inc. and Williams-Sonoma, Inc.

The recipes in this book have been previously published
in individual titles in the Williams-Sonoma Entertaining series.

All rights reserved, including the right of reproduction
in whole or in part in any form.

Color separations by Embassy Graphics
Printed and Bound in China by Toppan Leefung Printing Limited

First printed in 2010
10 9 8 7 6 5 4 3 2 1

Library of Congress Cataloging-in-Publication data is available.

ISBN-13: 978-1-4391-8686-2

ACKNOWLEDGMENTS

Weldon Owen wishes to thank Lisa Atwood, Ken della Penta,
Rachel Lopez Metzger, Tracy White, and Sharron Wood for their
generous support in producing this book.

This content was adapted from original recipes by
Georgeanne Brennan, George Dolese, and Lou Seibert Pappas.

PHOTOGRAPHY

Photographs by Quentin Bacon, Bill Bettencourt, Jim Franco,
John Granen, Keller & Keller, David Matheson, and Anna Williams.

JACKET IMAGES

Front cover: Lemon Custards with Lemon Verbena
Cream (page 67), Butter Lettuce and Herb Salad with
Dijon Vinaigrette (page 47), Herbed Pork Tenderloin
with Pancetta and Capers (page 188).

Back cover: Lamb Brochettes with Mint Gremolata
(page 124), Fried Artichokes with Aioli (page 32),
Iced Vin de Citron / Lemon Vodka Martinis (page 230),
Grilled Peaches with Toasted Almonds (page 139).